More Than Meatballs

From Arancini to Zucchini Fritters and 65 Recipes in Between

Michele Anna Jordan

**Foreword by
L. John Harris**

Photography by Liza Gershman

Skyhorse Publishing

Skyhorse Publishing books may be purchased in bulk at special discounts for sales promotion, corporate gifts, fund-raising, or educational purposes. Special editions can also be created to specifications. For details, contact the Special Sales Department, Skyhorse Publishing, 307 West 36th Street, 11th Floor, New York, NY 10018 or info@skyhorsepublishing.com.

Skyhorse® and Skyhorse Publishing® are registered trademarks of Skyhorse Publishing, Inc.®, a Delaware corporation.

Visit our website at www.skyhorsepublishing.com.

10 9 8 7 6 5 4 3 2 1

Library of Congress Cataloging-in-Publication Data is available on file.

Cover design by Brian Peterson
Cover photo credit: Liza Gershman

Print ISBN: 978-1-5107-1147-1
Ebook ISBN: 978-1-5107-1151-8

Printed in China

"Miracles are like meatballs, because nobody can exactly agree on what they are made of, where they come from, or how often they should appear."

—Lemony Snicket, *The Carnivorous Carnival*

for Mary Duryee

dear friend, patron, and the best home cook ever

for L. John Harris

my first publisher and editor, my friend, Garlic Guru, and Meatball Muse

&

for Andy Ross

my dear old friend and my fabulously brilliant new agent

Contents

Chapter 3: Going Meatless

Chapter 4: Context Is Everything

Appendix
Basic Recipes

Acknowledgments

When I think back on this time, the spring of 2014, I'll laugh as *Cloudy with a Chance of Meatballs* comes into focus in my mind's eye. I can't think of a better description for the process than a spaghetti and meatball tornado. What a whirlwind it has been, and a delicious one.

I am deeply grateful to Nicole Frail and her crew at Skyhorse Publishing for their patience, their kindness, and their speed.

And huge thanks, as well, to my agent, Andy Ross, for smoothing out all the contractual and deadline stuff and for introducing me to photographer Liza Gershman. Andy, you deserve a golden meatball.

To Liza, thank you so much, you little speed demon! Liza is a truly gifted photographer, with a phenomenal eye and an ability to work at what feels like warp speed. From our very first shots together, we've had a great intuitive and creative resonance that will carry us through many projects together. But first, let's raise a glass to *More Than Meatballs*! We did it! And now, onward to *Salt & Pepper* . . .

John Harris, thank you for everything over the years, and, especially, your inspired foreword.

Many thanks to Karen Martin, Marlena Spieler, and John Ash for sharing such yummy recipes.

I offer a big mahalo to Brooke Jackson, a hula sister and a colleague, for great help during our photo shoots. And to my teacher Kumu Hula Shawna Alapai'i, my uniki sisters and all of my hula sisters, mahalo nui loa for your support and understanding.

Jordan Rosenfeld, writer and radio colleague, thank you for "Have a Ball!"—a phrase that makes me want to kick up my heels and dance. It was right there, hanging over the project, but you were the one who plucked it from the ether and offered it up.

To my daughters, Gina and Nicolle, my grandson Lucas, my son-in-law Tom, and my dear friends John Boland and James Carroll, thank you thank you thank you, for everything, always.

Now, let's all have a ball!

Foreword

What goes around comes around. Meatballs! And here they are again in Michele Anna Jordan's new collection of meatball marvels, *More Than Meatballs.*

To be sure, these are all, despite their more than-ness, meat*balls*. And for good reason: try making a meatcube or a meatpyramid. Even the words look horribly wrong! No, the meatball is a gastronomic merger of form and function no less perfect than its relative, the wheel. Like I say, what goes around . . .

The only other cooked product of man's hungry genius that rivals the meatball for salutary simplicity and earthy economy is, I believe, the omelet. Curious though, omelets work inversely to the meatball: The omelet begins life round (the egg) and leaves it flat. The meatball starts its life flat (chopped meat, poultry, fish, etc.) and ends up round.

Of course there are flat-sided meatballs: sausage and hamburger patties and the monolithic American classic—meatloaf. These meatballish entities are what one observant aficionado of this class of foods, the eminent artist, writer and restaurateur, Daniel Spoerri, has labeled "the premasticated"—chopped animal-based foods. The ancient Persian word for meatball—*kufteh*—means "chopped."

Michele's meatballs, no matter how exuberantly chopped up with vegetables, grains, spices, herbs, and liquids, always maintain their rotund integrity. Balls.

Such esoteric reflections on the symbolism and morphology of the meatball are, nevertheless, beside the point when we are hungry and a well-made meatball or a dish containing well-made meatballs is placed in front of us. Like, for example, the meatball and pasta soup from Spain, Sopa de Albondigas y Fideo, from Michele's chapter titled (ironically) "Context Is Everything." The context here refers to meatballs in soups, salads, stews, and pastas.

I agree, context *is* everything. But I would add further that, for the humble meatball, the larger context is universal—hunger. One does not, dares not, approach a great meatball without hunger. We are, therefore, not talking here about *amuse bouche*–sized mini-meat-balls or *avant garde* molecular meatballs—rounded, gelatinized beef *jus*, as one might find on some trendy tasting menu in Barcelona or Copenhagen. That is not eating—that's entertainment. But neither are we talking mega meatballs for Monsieur Gargantua. Context is everything, and Michele's creations combine a feminine regard for both sensuality and sustenance on an appropriate scale designed for real eaters, not tasters.

Admittedly low on the trendy/foodie food chain of our day, the meatball is, at its core, more a strategy or methodology than a specific recipe, the poor man's way of using leftover cooked meat or uncooked meat and fat scraps. At least, that's the historical *raison d'etre* of the meatball. And like many humble dishes that emerged first as food of the poor, they are reinvented by new generations of aspiring cooks and eaters in search of simple, real food as an antidote to the fussy culinary fashions of the day (think Jewish pastrami or French *confit*). This is the rhythm of gastronomy through time, from simple to complex to simple again—a culinary circle.

Michele Anna Jordan's homage to the meatball is, to be sure, only the latest in a long, illustrious line of meatball compilations dating back to the ancient Roman cookbook *De re coquinaria* (*On the subject of cooking*), purportedly by a Roman gourmet named Apicius. But unlike Apicius's recipes in his chapter on "minces," Michele's approach to her subject is global, sophisticated, witty, imaginative, and *au courant*. Though, I should add, her rediscovery of caul fat (the digestive organ linings of cows, pigs, and sheep used, for example, as a casing for the traditional flat sausage patty in France known as the *crépinette*) as a perfect "cover up" for meatballs connects her back to ancient Apician minces wrapped in pork *omentum* (caul). Again, what goes around . . .

Which brings me back circuitously to another, less ancient treatment of the meatball and a very personal chapter from my days as publisher of cookbooks at Aris Books in the 1980s—the aforementioned Daniel Spoerri and his *Mythology & Meatballs: A Greek Island Diary/Cookbook* (Aris, 1982). This charmingly offbeat book not only introduced me to the meatball in all its global glory, but to the work of an important avant-garde European artist, writer, and proto-foodie.

Publishing Daniel Spoerri's culinary diary from his stay on the tiny Greek island of Symi, the closest Greek island to Turkey, in the 1960s—including his "A Dissertation on Keftedes" (*keftedes*, a Greek variation on the Persian *kufteh*)—was one of the highlights of my publishing career. This was food writing that transcended the genre and, long before I published the Aris edition, had in its original version, part of a larger non-culinary

French Sourdough
bread crumbs
moistened with
Spanish olive oil +
Petaluma Eggs

Mexican Red Garlic

Greek Oregano

New Zealand lamb
mixed with
Mid western Beef

CROSS SECTION
DIAMETER 1½"

Italian Parsley

Indian Black Pepper

Kosher Salt

"The Global Meatball (Keftedes *universalis*)" by L. John Harris, 1990

work, influenced my own first effort at food writing, *The Book of Garlic* (Holt, Rinehart, 1974).

Which in turn brings me back, like a rolling stone, to Michele, whose wonderful first cookbook, *A Cook's Tour of Sonoma*, we published in 1990—another highlight of my days at Aris. Ironically, one of my early "foodoodle" cartoons, titled "global meatball," was published in a local San Francisco Bay Area food magazine that same year. Little did Michele and I know in 1990 that we would come back together again professionally around the meatball.

It appears I have a karmic relationship with the meatball! And thanks to Michele Anna Jordan and her *More Than Meatballs*, I now have the pleasure of returning to a culinary subject near and dear to me. It may be too early to know whether Michele's book will launch a new meatball fad, or more likely, a meatball *movement*. But if it does, I will not be surprised. What goes around comes around, and when it is good, like Michele's meatball cookbook, it stays around.

L. John Harris
Paris, 2014

Introduction

"I love meatballs," friends declared when I told them what I was working on.
And then they giggled.
Sometimes they laughed first.

There is something inherently funny about *meatballs*, even the word itself. Maybe it's a memory of that old camp song. Given that most of us never got past the fourth line, let's give the old tune its due, shall we?

On top of spaghetti,
All covered with cheese,
I lost my poor meatball,
When somebody sneezed.

It rolled off the table,
And on to the floor,
And then my poor meatball,
Rolled out of the door.

It rolled in the garden,
And under a bush,
And then my poor meatball,
Was nothing but mush.

The mush was as tasty
As tasty could be,
And then the next summer,
It grew into a tree.

The tree was all covered,
All covered with moss,
And on it grew meatballs,
And tomato sauce.

So if you eat spaghetti,
All covered with cheese,
Hold on to your meatball,
Whenever you sneeze.

Sung to the tune of "On Top of Old Smokey," a traditional folk song of uncertain origin, "On Top of Spaghetti" was recorded by folksinger Tom Glazer with a chorus of children in 1963, though it appeared here and there in various publications as early as 1957.

The Meatball Muse is a jokester.

Meatballs is a 1979 film starring Bill Murray, a slang term for both a slovenly person and for intoxication, as in "I was totally *meatballed* by the end of that party."

Cloudy with a Chance of Meatballs is a popular animated film based on a children's book of the same name that involves an enormous tornado of spaghetti and meatballs, a giant meatball and a soundtrack with several meatball tunes, including "Outside the Meatball," "Inside the Meatball" and "The Heart of the Meatball," "Here's the Cheese," and, my favorite, "Meatier Shower."

According to Guinness World Records, the World's Largest Meatball was made by members of the Columbus Italian Club for their annual festival in October 2011. It weighed, initially, 1492 pounds but was certified at 1,110.5 pounds after three days of cooking. Samples of the meatball were offered at the festival on October 8, 2011, the date of certification. This Columbus, Ohio, group broke the previous record of a 759.5 pound meatball held by a German group. It did not go unnoticed that the raw weight of the meatball matched a very important number in history, 1492, the year Columbus sailed to the New World.

Although I've cooked meatballs for decades—almost always my favorite, roasted garlic meatballs—my interest was piqued near the end of 2011. Suddenly, food futurists, restaurant consultants, and others who earn their living anticipating trends declared that meatballs would be hot in 2012.

Clearly, something was up. The Meatball Shop, founded in Manhattan in 2010, was doing better than ever. Today it serves fifty-four types of meatballs at five New York City locations.

Cruisin' Kitchen, a New York food truck, is a partnership between Chef Keith Album and Marky Ramone, longtime drummer of the Ramones, who contributed his marinara sauce. The sauce is now produced commercially, bears a label with Ramone's logo and an image of Marky playing drums, and is sold in seven states and online.

Joey Ramone, the band's singer, recorded a provocative little tune, "Meatball Sandwich," with the band Youth Gone Mad before his death in April 2001.

Yes, meatballs are on a roll, a rock 'n' roll. Let's dance! *Let's have a ball!*

We live in an age of recipes, of precision, of concern over exact measurements and down-to-the-second timing. Cooking, to a large degree, is guided externally, by the written word, the video, the celebrity chef. It wasn't always this way. Indeed, this is a new attitude and, in many ways, a peculiarly American one. In just a couple of generations, we have forgotten how to cook intuitively, guided by a knowledge that is almost physical, absorbed during our youngest years at the side of a grandmother, an aunt, a mother who knew how to make everything taste good, meal after meal, day after day, year after year. It's not hard to get back there, back to simply cooking. Just start, don't take it too terribly seriously, learn from your mistakes and have fun.

You learn to cook, Julia Child said more than once, so you don't need to rely on recipes. I invite you to explore this book in that spirit. Please, enjoy my recipes. But at the same time, make them your own, and, please, *have a ball!*

Chapter 1

A Meatball Primer

You can make a good meatball out of almost any bit of meat. Add a few seasonings and a binder—something to make everything stick together—roll it up, and cook it however you like, fried in oil, boiled in water, soup or sauce, steamed in a bamboo basket. It will be pretty good.

It doesn't take more effort to make a *great* meatball but it does require putting thought into the ingredients and procuring the best you can. Today, markets are filled with greater variety and higher quality ingredients than at almost any time in our history. You can't find the very best ingredients by shopping exclusively in chain supermarkets and big box stores but discovering the alternative to these stores is an adventure in itself, a delightful one. There are thousands of farmers' markets in the United States and subscription farming is available in every state, including Alaska and Hawaii. Many farm subscriptions—typically known as CSA programs for "community supported agriculture"—offer eggs, cheese, poultry and meats in addition to the produce they grow. Some ranchers offer meat CSAs.

Here is my guide to both finding and selecting the ingredients that will make your meatballs soar.

Meat: It goes without saying that the most important ingredient in a meatball is the meat. It is important, *essential*, to understand and recognize good meat.

All meat should smell fresh and clean, with just a faint tang of iron. It should be uniformly colored, deep red for beef and lamb, paler but not too pale for pork. It is best wrapped in paper, not plastic. If you buy plastic-wrapped meat, remove it as soon as you get home and rewrap it in wax paper.

If meat is discolored, slimy or smelly, either don't buy it or return it to the store.

The very best meat will come from a source near you, a local or regional ranch, preferably one that raises grass-fed meats. There is abundant evidence that grass-fed meats are better—nutritionally and environmentally—than meats from animals fed a corn-based diet or finished on corn. When you cannot get local or regional meat, find a butcher shop and cultivate a relationship with the butcher, who will know the best sources and the best cuts for whatever it is you are preparing.

Avoid meat from large factory farms, don't buy meat from big box stores and, when it comes to pork, look for meat from heritage breeds.

"They've ruined pork," Julia Child said to me one afternoon at a local winery, "and now they are trying to ruin beef, too."

Julia was referring, of course, to lean pork, which should be an oxymoron but isn't. Factory farms now raise lean pigs and advertising campaigns boast about this low-fat meat. But pigs are not lean animals and their fat is essential to both their own health and the meat they produce. Small ranchers throughout the country are raising heritage breeds but if you can't find such meat use pork shoulder or butt for meatballs, never loin, and do not remove any of the fat. If you don't want to grind it yourself, ask your butcher and find another butcher shop if your request is not honored.

Lamb can be difficult to find, especially if you live in the South, where it has never been a staple. In such areas, Whole Foods is a good source. If you don't see it, ask someone at the meat counter to order it for you. Shoulder cuts are best for meatballs; if you use leg, be sure to include extra fat.

Goat is increasingly available in America, especially in areas where goat cheese is produced. Latin markets are a good source for goat meat, as are farmers' markets. Goat from young animals is mild, flavorful, easy to cook and delicious. It makes *great* meatballs.

A word about veal is essential, too, as it has long been a traditional ingredient in meatballs. However, cruel husbandry practices make veal a marginal choice. Practices have improved in recent years—there is now range-fed veal—but I have avoided it for decades and continue to do so because I have found it difficult to know its source with confidence.

Poultry: It is every bit as important, if not more so, to find chicken raised close to home, preferably outside on pasture. Commodity chicken is a cruel business that produces an inferior product, chicken with little flavor and an unpleasant almost mushy texture. We have hundreds of small chicken farmers in the United States and it is increasingly easy to find pastured chicken. In the last few years, air-chilled chicken has become the norm and it is a great improvement over the ice-water system that has been used for decades. Ice baths

dilute flavor and add water weight to the chicken so choose air-chilled whenever you have the option.

For duck and turkey, my advice is the same. Look for birds raised outdoors close to home.

For our purposes, for the purposes of meatballs, use thigh and leg meat. Breast meat is too lean and, when it comes to chicken and turkey, takes on an unpleasant flavor during lengthy cooking. I find it helpful to add extra fat when I grind poultry for meatballs; this fat keeps the meat lubricated as it cooks, which results in juicy meatballs.

Fat: Fat is so crucial to making good meatballs that it warrants its own section. Fat is not, as we have been led to believe, our enemy. Eating it will not make us fat. Fat, particularly the fat of ruminants, has essential nutrients that are hard or impossible to get from other sources. When it comes to meatballs, fat's primary roles are to lubricate ingredients as they cook and to distribute flavors. No matter what meat you are using for meatballs, you want a minimum of 15 percent fat; 20 to 25 percent fat is better. Much of this fat will melt as the meatball cooks but this action, the draining away, is essential, as flavors are distributed and ingredients lubricated as the fat melts.

Because everything—nutrients, antibiotics, hormones, pesticides and other toxins—concentrates in an animal's fat, it is important to choose fat, including butter, from pastured, grass-fed and, when possible, organic meats.

Salt: Salt is the most essential seasoning in meatballs and in just about everything else. Without salt, flavors do not blossom fully and our palates do not engage with them completely. If you omit salt from a recipe that calls for it, you will likely be disappointed with the outcome.

It is best to salt in stages, seasoning, say, onions, shallots and garlic before adding other ingredients, adding a bit more salt after the meat has been mixed in and making a final adjustment just before finishing a dish. If you salt only at the end of the cooking process, you will likely use more salt in a futile attempt to get flavors to blossom.

I rely primarily on two salts. Diamond Crystal Kosher Salt is my default salt, the one I use in daily cooking. It has a dry flake that is easy to grab with my fingers and it dissolves quickly, bringing flavors with it as it does. It is inexpensive so you won't cringe when tossing a handful into a big pot of water for pasta.

I also use Maldon Salt Flakes, a salt that is similar to Diamond Crystal Kosher Salt, which is to say it is a very dry flake that dissolves quickly. Its larger flakes make it a great finishing salt. Because it is produced in England in small batches, it is fairly expensive and thus impractical to use as a cooking salt.

Other Seasonings: Pepper is almost as essential to meatballs as salt and it is best to grind it at the last minute. Nearly half of the flavor of black pepper is contained in the outer mantle and begins to dissipate as soon as that mantle is cracked, which is why ground pepper has a one-dimensional taste. In much of the world, people cook with white pepper and use black pepper to finish a dish at the last minute. I recommend this, though I have given up being a proselytizer because white pepper just isn't that common in the United States.

Crushed red pepper flakes belong in many meatballs and the better the brand, the more flavor they will contribute. I prefer Mammarella Foods crushed red pepper flakes, a brand owned by Francis Ford Coppola. They have the fullest flavor of any commercial brand I've tasted and are widely available.

For other spices, I use local suppliers that grind their own spices. See Resources, page 183, for my recommendations.

Fillers: Meatballs typically include some sort of filler, a tradition that arose from the meatball's history as peasant food. When you have little meat, you need fillers to keep the family fed.

But are they essential to the taste of the meatball?

Not really. You can make amazingly good meatballs without any filler.

Most fillers honor tradition and create a taste, texture, and heft we recognize. But a meatball cooks perfectly and tastes great without fillers. I say this with one qualification. When you use meat with a low percentage of fat, a filler may help keep the meatball succulent by absorbing juices that might otherwise drain away.

If you wish to use a bread filler, use good fresh bread or hearth bread that is just a few days old. Stale bread, commercial bread crumbs or crushed Saltine crackers often result in dry meatballs, though a good home cook will not have this problem.

Today, there is another consideration, gluten-intolerance. More and more people are finding they feel better if they don't eat gluten, and celiac disease, a hypersensitivity to gluten that causes inflammation and interferes with digestion, is on the rise, too. There are

Using Caul Fat

Stretch caul fat as thinly as possible on a clean wooden work surface.

It is not necessary to cut off the caul fat as you stretch it; simply leave it in a ball and pull it out as needed. It is fairly sturdy, not at all as delicate as it appears.

Use a melon baller or ice cream scoop to form your meatball.

Set the meatball on the edge of the caul fat, leaving a margin around it for wrapping.

Once you are comfortable with the process, form several balls at a time before cutting the caul fat.

Wrap the caul fat around the entire meatball, pulling it as thinly as possible without ripping it.

After each meatball is wrapped, use a sharp knife to cut around it.

Be sure the meatball is completely encased in caul fat.

plenty of options, beyond simply omitting the filler. Many traditional meatballs, those of Greece, for example, call for rice instead of bread. Some cuisines incorporate oats. Quinoa, a seed typically used as we use grain, is an excellent filler, too.

Although I make specific recommendations for fillers in this book, you should feel free to use what you prefer. If you avoid gluten, experiment with rice, quinoa or steel-cut oats to discover what you prefer. I don't recommend searching for gluten-free bread crumbs or such; it's too much trouble and these other ingredients work better anyway.

Binders: When making meatballs, you need something to bind the meat together. The single most common binder is the egg, which also adds a richness to the mix. For the best results, use local pastured eggs from a farm stand or farmers' market. Some experts claim that this is merely an environmental act, that there is no difference in taste between a factory egg and an egg from a happy pastured hen. A single bite should reveal this is not accurate. Factory eggs are bland and watery, with little true egg flavor. Pastured eggs are luscious, rich, delicious and deeply satisfying.

Many home cooks once used canned condensed milk to help bind their meatballs but today nearly all condensed milk is sweetened. I do not recommend it.

Binders have a secondary function and that is to moisten the meatball and keep it juicy. In addition to eggs, I recommend roasted garlic purée, steamed zucchini, and eggplant, though not all in one meatball, of course. But each of these ingredients keeps meatballs succulent and helps to distribute flavors. If you have been troubled by dry meatballs, one of these ingredients should offer a delicious solution.

Word About Cheese: Cheese is typically included in meatballs in cuisines where cheese is part of the culture. It is common in the meatballs of Western Europe but rarely if ever found in Asian meatballs.

The function of cheese touches on three categories, fat, binder and filler. By definition, cheese contributes fat. Some cheeses help bind ingredients together, some—such as whole milk ricotta—lighten the meatball and increase its bulk, creating a lusciously delicate sphere.

Some cheeses work well as stuffing, too, which is easy to accomplish. All you do is insert a little nugget into the center of a meatball and make sure the mixture is closed tightly around the cheese.

Coatings: Once we've gone to the trouble of securing the best possible meat, seasoned it perfectly, added pastured eggs to hold it all together and carefully put in just enough quinoa to create the perfect bulk, we must decide how to finish the meatball.

Should we simply cook it, without coating it first?

That is certainly an option and a good one. It is not absolutely necessary to cloak a meatball in anything before cooking.

Yet there are advantages. With the right coating, you can add an outer snap and inner succulence to your meatball. And in the case of most fritters and croquettes, coating is essential for the roundness to hold.

Coatings include flour, egg, dry bread crumbs, fresh bread crumbs, the Japanese bread crumbs known as Panko or a combination of these ingredients. In this book, I offer several options recipe by recipe.

Wrappings: This is where you can make your meatballs stand out from all the others and, at the same time, honor the ancient tradition of Marcus Gavius Apicius, a gourmand who is said to have lived in ancient Rome in the first century. *De Re Coquinaria* ("The Art of Cooking"), the earliest known collection of recipes, is credited to him. Book II of the ten-book series is about meatballs, or minces, as he called them.

"Ground meat patties in omentum" is how Apicius described what we now call meatballs and they were simply chopped meat—from peacock, pheasant, rabbit, chicken or pork—with a few seasonings, wrapped in a thin membrane that we know as caul fat.

As I experimented with recipes for this book, I became smitten with caul fat, in part because I had tasted a simple crépinette of ground venison wrapped in caul fat years ago and thought it would be a great way to encase a meatball. I hadn't considered putting it into a general cookbook, though, because until quite recently, caul fat existed primarily in the domain of professional chefs. It was simply not possible to buy a small amount. But with the renaissance of whole animal butchery that is under way in the United States, that has changed. Where I live, there are several retail sources for whatever amount of caul fat I want. It is also readily available online.

Caul fat is a membrane of fat that encloses the organs of the four-legged creatures we eat. It stretches out very thin and resembles, more than anything, a lace curtain. A pound sells for about three or four dollars and is enough to wrap several dozen meatballs. It's a bargain. It's always easy to use, much easier than, say, rolling a meatball first in flour, then in beaten egg and then in breadcrumbs, as many recipes advise.

A meatball wrapped in caul fat cooks a tad differently, too. It loses less liquid and takes on a succulent quality that meatballs coated in flour and crumbs lack. It is now my preferred way to prepare meatballs.

I fell in love with caul fat without realizing its ancient roots and when I did discover that Apicius wrapped his meatballs in caul fat, it felt like a blessing, especially since it was my dear friend John Harris's foreword to this book that enlightened me.

You'll find a source for caul fat in Resources, page 183.

A Happy Kitchen: You don't need a luxurious kitchen to cook well. In my experience, the best home cooking typically comes from modest kitchens, kitchens with stained and marred cutting boards, wooden spoons scarred by flame, pots and pans blackened with age. So-called luxury kitchens, the ones that are bigger than many houses, with eight burner commercial ranges, marble counters, every imaginable tool and floors that are cleaner than my countertops suggest the sort of privilege that does not require actual cooking. These kitchens are mostly for show and for the private chefs and caterers who occasionally prepare a meal in them. If you have a humble little kitchen, embrace it and fill it with exactly what you need and nothing more.

The most important part of any kitchen is its **lighting**, which, if you are very lucky, floods in from a window over the sink during the day. When you can't see your ingredients, cooking is a challenge. If you have poor light fixtures but can't replace them, consider one or two carefully placed table lamps. I have one on top of my refrigerator, with the light focused on the nearby stove, which it illuminates perfectly.

One or two large wooden cutting boards are essential. Wood has natural antibacterial properties, is easier on knives than plastic boards and possesses a natural beauty. Plastic cutting boards, even after being sent through a commercial dishwasher, retain substantial amounts of bacteria. Although health departments all over the country began requiring them in commercial kitchens in the 1980s, they have since backed off, as study after study confirm that food-grade hardwood is better.

Two high-quality knives are essential, too. Nothing hinders a cook or renders cooking an unpleasant chore like a dull knife. At a minimum, you need a non-serrated paring knife and an all-purpose chef's knife, purchased at a specialty shop that allows you to explore several brands. It is important to select knives with handles that fit comfortably in *your* hand, so that your hand will neither tire quickly nor cramp as you use it. Resist the urge to buy cheap knives, even those with brand names at big box stores. They are not the same as those sold in specialty shops. Pony up for the real thing and you will be glad you did. You'll need to learn to sharpen it, too, so ask your knife vendor to show you how or ask if they offer free annual sharpening; many do.

A meat grinder is a handy tool to have in your meatball arsenal, as grinding your own meat has many advantages. If you already own a Kitchen Aid Mixer, a grinder attachment is the best way to go. It's efficient, inexpensive, easy to use, easy to clean and doesn't take up much space; I store mine in the bowl of my mixer.

If you do not have a Kitchen Aid Mixer, you'll want a manual grinder. It attaches to your kitchen counter by means of a large screw, it opens up for easy cleaning and it is are almost indestructible. I have an old one that belonged to my mother and to her mother before her.

I find a **suribachi**—a Japanese mortar and pestle—essential. It consists of a porcelain bowl scored on the inside to facilitate grinding and crushing and a wooden pestle. Use it to crush garlic, herbs, cilantro roots and such and to grind spices. It is easy to clean, inexpensive and does not require electricity. The best source is an Asian market.

If you love to cook, get a **mandoline**, a mechanic device that creates uniform slices in varying widths, from thin julienne to wide rounds. You don't need a professional model; a simple plastic one, such as a Zyliss or OXO, will do all you need it to do for years and, if handled properly, decades. Japanese mandolines are excellent, too; look for them in Asian markets.

I'm not a big fan of nonstick pans but I keep one around for meatballs. After experimenting with several types, I have found a ceramic-coated nonstick pan produces the best results. Whatever pans you use should have heavy bottoms that conduct heat evenly, without hotspots. Cast iron skillets and Dutch ovens are always excellent and last forever, or nearly so. When I buy new pans, I typically choose All-Clad; this brand conducts heat well, is easy to clean and has handles that fit my hand comfortably.

I recommend a **kitchen scale**, preferably an electronic one. I have an OXO scale that weighs up to 11 pounds and I use it several times a day. It is much more efficient and accurate–and much easier, once you get the hang of it–to weigh ingredients than it is to measure their volume.

Ice cream scoops and **melon ballers** make forming meatballs of uniform size easy. I have several, from ¾ ounce to 2 ounces.

It goes without saying, or should, that any kitchen should be equipped with a set of dry measuring cups and spoons, at least one liquid measuring cup, a sturdy vegetable peeler and sturdy wooden spoons with thick rather than spindly handles, along with a lot of glass bowls of varying sizes for holding ingredients as you prepare them. Flexible rubber spatulas are essential for scraping ingredients out of containers and you must have tongs for turning meatballs and transferring them from one vessel to another. You'll want a large slotted spoon for lifting fritters and croquettes out of simmering oil.

Necessary Skills: If you don't know how to hold a knife properly, learn. Many cooks have a habit of using the index finger of their dominant hand to steady a knife but this is a *bad* habit, not a desirable one. All four fingers and your thumb should wrap around a knife's handle, which is the reason you should select a knife that is comfortable to hold. It is your grip that will keep the knife steady, not a finger on the back of the blade.

It is important, as well, to know what to do with your non-dominant hand as you prepare your ingredients. You *must* keep it out of the way. You can use the hand to feed ingredients to the knife, always keeping your fingers rolled under so that you do not accidentally cut them and moving the ingredients, not the knife. For the best control, keep the knife in one spot and move the ingredients towards the blade as you cut. Master this technique and you will have tremendous control in the kitchen.

It is important, as well, to select the right tools for the right task. Amateur cooks tend to think small, by which I mean they tend to think of the smallest container that will hold what needs to be held or the smallest surface possible to complete a task. The opposite is better. Using larger work surfaces and containers than you think you'll need will give you room to work and your ingredients room to expand. A small dish is perfect for holding, say, garlic puree until it is tipped into a larger container of ingredients but mixing together several ingredients is best accomplished in a roomy vessel.

Don't be afraid of heat and don't worry when something sticks at first. When cooking meatballs, you want to sear the outside quickly, which requires substantial heat. When you put meatballs into a hot pan, don't move them right away. Instead, cook them for at least 45 seconds before agitating the pan. If they stick, be patient: A little more time on the heat and they will loosen right up and roll cooperatively.

Common Sense Food Safety: I eat meat rare and sometimes raw, I think it is a crime to cook an oyster and I use raw eggs in everything from Caesar salad and home-made mayonnaise to steak tartare. If a hamburger is cooked beyond rare, I'm not interested and, yes, I'll send it back.

Yet every day it seems there is a new warning that puts caution before pleasure, before taste, before tradition and before common sense. Better safe than sorry, we are told. Eat an egg over easy and who knows what terrible fate might befall you. In the 1980s, the State of New Jersey even made it illegal for restaurants to serve eggs with runny yolks, a prohibition that lasted about seven days before the ordinance was reversed.

Is the modern world really so dangerous and, if so, why?

Large-scale factory farming is the culprit. If you pay attention to recalls and food-borne illnesses, if you trace the causes to their source, you almost always find a large-scale operation. When, for example, ground beef is tainted with e-coli, it typically involves a dozen or more states and meat that comes, literally, from *hundreds* of animals.

When eggs and meat are produced on a large scale, animals live in truly appalling conditions. When they meet their fate, slaughtered carcasses tumble against each other, making contamination by intestinal contents all but inevitable. The very best hedge against food-borne illnesses from eggs and meat is to buy local or as locally as possible. Don't procure these foods from big box stores but do try to cultivate a relationship with a local butcher who will take the time to talk to you about sources and husbandry practices.

The same approach is best for fruits and vegetables. Tainted cantaloupe, sprouts, lettuce, strawberries: The problem is never the farm down the road. It's the farm six states east or west or, in some instances, halfway around the globe. Tainted frozen fruit sold at Costco a few years ago came, in part, from Turkey.

Government advisories and recommendations typically infantilize our population, speaking to the lowest common denominator and assuming that, well, Americans are simply not that smart. For example, recently there was a rash of recommendations advising that chicken should not be rinsed before it is cooked.

Why?

Because of the possibility of cross contamination, presumably because whomever is rinsing that chicken under cool running water—a process that removes liquid that has leached from the chicken and can contribute off flavors and dilute sauce—is too dumb to move the lettuce or the tomatoes out from under it or simply not put them there in the first place.

Food safety is, first and foremost, a matter of common sense. If you want to rinse that chicken, move the vegetables! Don't leave proteins at room temperature for too long. Wash your cutting boards, knives and hands frequently. Clean up as you go.

When it comes to meat, if you have a local source, use it. If you don't have a local source, find a good butcher shop or market with a butcher counter. Ask them to grind meat for you or buy what they grind in house, from a single source, i.e., one cut of meat, one animal. Contamination happens most readily when dozens of recently slaughtered carcasses are tumbled together.

Why These Recipes & Not Others? About halfway through writing the first draft of this book, I realized two things. First of all, I understood it would not be possible to represent every type of meatball in the world. There are too many, endless variations on the theme of a bit of chopped up meat rolled into a ball with a few seasonings, a binder and, frequently, something that stretches the quantity. I set out, initially, to offer a representative sample of meatballs from around the world but soon realized this was not the wisest approach. I culled those included merely as an example of, say, a technique or style and selected, instead, meatballs that I love and enjoy serving to family and friends. I employed my preferred techniques and ingredients, abandoning traditional additions and methods when I believed—and hoped—my approach would make a better meatball.

A Few Words About Wine: I live in the heart of one of America's premier wine regions, the Russian River Valley appellation, itself a part of the Sonoma County appellation, home to dozens of unique microclimates and hundreds of wineries. Wine is an automatic part of daily life here. But there's more, extraordinary small craft breweries, artisan distilleries and new hard ciders facilities that are reviving an early American craft. Johnny Appleseed did not plant apple trees for apple pies or applesauce; he planted trees that produce small tart fruit perfect for cider, once the most common beverage in America, even for children, because it was more wholesome—cleaner—than most of the country's drinking water. In this book, I have made beverage suggestions where I think my recommendations will enhance the dish and your pleasure as you enjoy it.

Chapter 2

Delicious Traditions and Contemporary Customs

To paraphrase the famous first line of Tolstoy's *Anna Karenina,* with all due apologies, all good meatballs are alike; each bad meatball is bad in its own way. A good meatball is moist, juicy, tender, chewy, flavorful and perfectly balanced. A bad meatball might have no taste, it might be so dry you can't swallow it without a big slug of water, it may be so sweet it tastes like dessert. It might be mushy, a quality that makes me shudder.

There are many ways a meatball can go wrong but they are not our concern.

Follow these recipes or simply take inspiration from them and I guarantee you nothing but yummy meatballs.

America is a land of plenty, including plenty of meatballs, as wave after wave of immigrants have brought them—not literally, of course, but as recipes, *as memories*—from their homeland. In Solvang, California, a town known for its Danish heritage, you'll find frikadeller—veal and pork meatballs in brown gravy—on the menu of the Solvang Brewing Company. As Minnesota celebrates its Scandinavian heritage, Swedish meatballs have become increasingly available. Every community with a Chinese population has a selection of dim sum balls, some with meat, others with fish and shellfish, others with a combination. There are Mexican and Spanish albondigas, Portuguese almondegas, French boules and boulettes de viande, Turkish kofte, Italian polpette and polpettini and so many more, too many to name.

Yet despite the remarkable array of meatballs in America, a single one took hold, insinuating itself not only into our homes and our food industry but into our very language. Say "meatball" and it is the Italian polpette that comes to mind. In the 1950s and '60s, millions of kids grew up on Chef Boyardee Spaghetti & Meatballs right out of the can. A lot of us can't think of a single meatball that isn't Italian.

That's where I come in.

In this chapter, I do, of course, pay homage to our Italian meatball. Yet I offer many other favorites, some from tradition and history, others from my travels, some from my own repertoire, influenced by my native California, where Italian, Mexican, and French influences shaped both my palate and my cooking.

At some point as I worked and reworked recipes and discovered new variations, I realized I would have to alter my approach a bit. Instead of treating meatballs as I might approach a survey of world literature, with a little bit of everything, the best from around the world, as I did at first, I realized, *remembered*, that culinary traditions are born of need, of geography, and of isolation. Most cultures have some sort of meatball and the variations have to do not with quality but with traditional ingredients and tools, in turn a reflection of climate and location. It became increasingly clear, like fog lifting to reveal a landscape or steam dispersing to unveil a skilletful of yummy albondigas, that it would be better to focus on the ingredients, methods, and techniques that I believe make the best meatballs. That is what I have done throughout the book, including in this chapter.

As I explored the world's meatballs, one in particular, a *badduzze*, caught my attention as I was reading *Pomp and Sustenance: Twenty-Five Centuries of Sicilian Food* (Alfred A. Knopf, New York, 1989) by Mary Taylor Simeti. The recipe itself is simple enough: chopped meat, typically veal or beef, with bread crumbs, eggs, cheese, garlic, and salt and pepper, which pretty much sums up all meatballs everywhere. The unique element is how the *badduzze* is cooked. Each little ball is pressed between two leaves of an orange tree or lemon tree—both are ubiquitous in Sicily—and then grilled over coals. The fire releases the essential oil in the leaves which in turn permeates the meat. Yum. If you have a citrus tree, definitely give this technique a try.

It is important, I think, to address size, as it does matter with meatballs. I don't think anyone would call my meatballs diminutive, exactly, though they do tend to run on the small side. I like a meatball that I can pop into my mouth whole or devour in no more than two bites. This size has, I think, the perfect ratio of interior to exterior. Once a meatball is big enough to require slicing, it moves toward meatloaf even as it retains its shape. It loses the many charms and advantages that come with being bite-sized. A small meatball has a certain femininity about it, a girly quality. Big meatballs are, by definition, rather messy and, I might add, macho. Smallish meatballs fit neatly, *politely*, on sandwiches and in tortillas. In soup, small meatballs make a perfect spoonful. I could go on but I think I have made my case. But if you don't agree with me, that's okay; simply make your meatballs bigger than I suggest.

The Meatball

Makes about 32 small or 16 large meatballs

Here it is, The Meatball, an Americanized Italian immigrant, the one meatball deserving of the unmodified moniker, the meatball everyone thinks of when they hear the word. This specific recipe has evolved over my decades of simply cooking, first as a sixteen-year-old bride, then as a chef, and now as grandmother of Lucas, thirteen, who was born with a precise and adventurous palate and loves *these meatballs.*

1 cup torn white bread, from sturdy hearth
    bread, preferably sourdough
¾ cup milk or white wine
1 pound grass-fed beef, ground twice
1 pound pastured pork, ground twice
1 small yellow onion, grated
3 garlic cloves, minced
3 tablespoons chopped fresh Italian parsley
¾ cup (3 ounces) grated Parmigiano-
    Reggiano, Dry Jack, or similar cheese

Kosher salt
Black pepper in a mill
½–1 teaspoon red pepper flakes, to taste
Whole nutmeg
2 large pastured eggs, beaten
1 cup fresh bread crumbs (page 173), or
    6 ounces caul fat
Olive oil

Put the bread and milk or wine into a mixing bowl and use a fork to crush the bread and blend it into the liquid. Set aside for about 15 minutes.

Add the beef, pork, onion, garlic, Italian parsley, and cheese to the bowl and mix well. Season generously with salt, several turns of black pepper, red pepper flakes, and several gratings of nutmeg and mix again. Add the eggs, mix well, and then knead for a minute or two until very well blended.

Cover and refrigerate for at least an hour or as long as overnight.

To finish, cover a sheet pan with wax paper.

Use a 1-ounce ice cream scoop to form small meatballs or a 2-ounce scoop to make larger meatballs; set each ball on the wax paper.

If using bread crumbs, put them into a mixing bowl, add a meatball, and agitate the bowl to coat the meatball well. Set it on a baking sheet and continue until all are coated.

If using caul fat, spread the fat on a clean work surface and wrap each ball, as described on page 8.

To cook, pour a thin film of olive oil on a heavy skillet set over medium-high heat. When the pan is hot, add several meatballs, being certain not to crowd them. Cook for about 45 seconds and then agitate the pan so the balls roll. Continue cooking until the balls are evenly browned and have begun to firm up, about 5 to 7 minutes, depending on their size. Set the cooked balls on absorbent paper and continue until all have been cooked.

To serve neat, return the meatballs to the pan, reduce the heat to very low, cover, and cook for 4 to 5 minutes for small meat balls and about 12 minutes for large ones, until the meatballs are just cooked through. Transfer to a platter and serve hot.

> **Serving Suggestions:** In classic Spaghetti & Meatballs, with marinara sauce; in traditional lasagna; in soups; on sliders and sandwiches.

Roasted Garlic Meatballs

Makes about 32 meatballs

If I had to pick just one meatball to cook for the rest of my life, it likely would be this one. I've made it for many years and served it in a wide array of contexts—as an appetizer, in sandwiches and tacos, over spaghettini with the juices from roasting the garlic. My first batch ever resulted in 750 1-inch meatballs, each one stuffed, by hand, with a single clove of roasted and peeled garlic. After that grueling extravaganza, I said never again and began mixing roasted garlic purée directly into the meat mixture. This is the not-so-secret ingredient that gives the meatball its luscious texture. Since I began wrapping these in caul fat, these yummy morsels have gotten even better.

3 tablespoons olive oil
2 shallots, peeled and minced
8 garlic cloves, minced
Kosher salt
Black pepper in a mill
1 pound grass-fed beef, ground twice
1 pound pastured pork, ground twice

¾ cup roasted garlic purée (page 176)
½ cup minced fresh Italian parsley
6 ounces Dry Jack or similar cheese, grated
1½ cups steamed quinoa
3 eggs, beaten
4 to 5 ounces caul fat

Heat 2 tablespoons of the olive oil in a small sauté pan set over medium-low heat, add the shallots and cook until soft and fragrant, about 7 minutes; do not let them brown. Add the minced garlic and sauté 1 minute more. Season with salt and pepper and set aside to cool.

Put the ground beef and pork in a medium bowl, add the cooled shallot mixture, garlic purée, parsley, cheese, and quinoa. Season generously with salt and pepper, add the eggs and mix thoroughly with your hands until a smooth mixture has formed. Refrigerate for at least 30 minutes or as long as overnight.

To finish the meatballs, cover a sheet pan with wax paper.

Use a 1-ounce ice cream scoop to form balls and set them on the wax paper.

Wrap each one in caul fat, as described on page 8.

When all the balls have been wrapped, set a heavy skillet over medium-high heat, add the remaining tablespoon of olive oil and, when the pan is hot, add several of the meatballs. Cook for about 30 seconds and then agitate the pan so that the balls roll; cook 30 seconds more and agitate the pan again. Cook until the balls have firmed up a bit; return them to the wax paper, and continue until all the balls have been browned.

To serve neat, return all of the meatballs to the pan, lower the heat as much as possible, cover the pan and cook very gently for about 12 minutes or until just cooked through. To test, press on a meatball; if it feels somewhat firm, it is done.

Transfer to a platter and serve immediately, with toothpicks and condiments of choice.

> **Serving Suggestions:** As an appetizer, with crème fraîche for dipping; in classic Spaghetti & Meatballs; spaghetti with Summer Tomato Sauce; with spaghettini tossed with the liquid from roasting garlic and grated cheese.

Roasted Garlic Meatballs

Bolognese-Style Goat Meatballs

Makes about 24 small meatballs

Goat meat has, in recent years, become more accepted by mainstream Americans and more readily available. If you live in an area where goat cheese is made, for example, you should have easy access to goat meat, as well. Meat from young goat is full-flavored, with a pleasing richness and none of that "goaty" taste that some people find objectionable in older goat meat. If you can't find it or don't want to use it, you can use beef instead without making any other adjustments. If you happen to have venison or bison, all the better; both are delicious in this recipe.

2 tablespoons butter

2 tablespoons grated yellow onion

2 garlic cloves, minced

Kosher salt

Black pepper in a mill

½ teaspoon ground cardamom

Whole nutmeg

1 pound goat shoulder or leg, ground twice

½ pound mortadella, ground once

2 tablespoons chopped fresh Italian parsley

¾ cup grated (3 ounces) cheese, such as Laura Chenel Tome, Romano-Pecorino, or similar hard cheese

1 duck egg or 2 small chicken eggs, beaten

3 to 4 ounces caul fat

2 tablespoons olive oil

Put the butter into a small sauté pan set over medium-low heat and, when the butter is melted, add the onion and sauté 4 or 5 minutes until it is fragrant; do not let it brown. Add the garlic, sauté 1 minute more, season generously with salt, several turns of black pepper, the cardamom, and 2 or 3 gratings of nutmeg. Remove from the heat and let cool.

Put the ground goat meat and the ground mortadella into a mixing bowl, add the cooled onion mixture along with the parsley, cheese, and egg. Mix thoroughly, cover, and refrigerate for at least an hour or as long as overnight.

To finish, cover a sheet pan with wax paper.

Use a 1-ounce ice cream scoop to form balls and set each ball on the wax paper.

Spread caul fat on a clean work surface and wrap each ball in a thin layer of it (see page 8); return each wrapped ball to the wax paper.

Pour the olive oil into a large heavy skillet set over medium-high heat and, when the pan is hot, add several meatballs, being certain not to crowd them. Cook for 45 seconds, agitate the pan so that the balls roll, and continue to cook until they are evenly browned and beginning to firm up.

Transfer the finished balls to absorbent paper and continue until all have been cooked.

To serve neat, as an appetizer, return the balls to the skillet, set the heat on very low, cover the pan, and simmer very gently until cooked through, about 4 to 5 minutes. Remove from the heat, transfer to a plate or bowl, and serve immediately.

Alternately, use these meatballs in another recipe.

> **Serving Suggestions:** Over pappardelle, with a traditional ragu; in lasagna; in white bean soup; in sliders, sandwiches, and tacos.

Sicilian-Inspired Balls

Makes about 36 small meatballs

Raisins, sweet Marsala, and citrus are common ingredients in Sicily, including in savory dishes. I like the flavors these ingredients contribute best when there is a hint of smoke, as there is in the cheese I use—smoked Caciocavallo. It is available in Italian markets in major cities and can be purchased through many websites, as well.

¼ cup golden raisins
3 tablespoons Marsala
2 cups, lightly packed, hearth bread,
    without crusts, torn into small pieces
½ cup whole milk or cream
3 to 4 garlic cloves, crushed and minced
2 teaspoons grated orange zest
2 teaspoons grated lemon zest
¾ pound freshly ground beef
¾ pound freshly ground pork
¼ cup pine nuts, lightly toasted
2 tablespoons chopped Italian parsley

Pinch of cinnamon
2 eggs, beaten
2 ounces smoked Caciocavallo or similar
    cheese, grated
Kosher salt
Black pepper in a mill
6 ounces caul fat
1 tablespoon olive oil
1 orange, cut in thin rounds
1 lemon, cut in thin rounds
3 tablespoons thinly sliced mint

Put the raisins into a small bowl, add the Marsala, and set aside.

Put the bread into a small saucepan, add the milk and the garlic, and warm over low heat. When all the milk has been absorbed by the bread, smash the bread with a fork to create a sort of slurry or mush. Stir in the orange zest and lemon zest and set aside to cool.

When the raisins have become plump, drain off the Marsala and set both aside.

Put the pork and beef into a mixing bowl, add the cooled bread mixture, the pine nuts, the raisins, the parsley, and the cinnamon and mix well. Add the eggs and the cheese and season generously with salt and pepper; mix thoroughly.

Cover and refrigerate at least 1 hour or as long as overnight.

To finish, cover a baking sheet with wax paper.

Set the caul fat on a clean work surface.

Use a 1-ounce ice cream scoop to form balls and set each ball on the wax paper.

When all the balls are made, wrap each one in caul fat (see page 8).

To cook, pour the olive oil into a heavy skillet set over medium-high heat and, when the pan is hot, add several meatballs. Cook for 45 seconds, agitate the pan so that the balls roll, and continue cooking until they are evenly browned all over and beginning to firm up. Return all the balls to the skillet, reduce the heat to low, add the reserved Marsala, and cook for 3 to 4 minutes, until the meatballs are just cooked through.

Spread the orange and lemon slices over a platter, set the meatballs on top, sprinkle with mint, and serve immediately.

> **Serving Suggestions:** As an appetizer; as a main course with caponata or with simple grilled eggplant and roasted peppers; on sandwiches with marinara sauce and Caciocavallo melted under a broiler.

Barcelona Balls

Makes about 24 meatballs

Call them Boles de Picolat or Catalan meatballs if you like, but my version, inspired in part by Colman Andrews's evocative writing on the topic in Catalan Cuisine: Europe's Last Great Culinary Secret *(Grub Street, 1997), is named in honor of one of the world's most glorious cities, Barcelona, where I have enjoyed some of the best meals of my life. The rustic food of the region, not its avant-garde molecular cuisine, has most enchanted me. The delicious nibbles at tiny bars in the Boqueria and leisurely lunches in the Gothic quarter and out-of-the-way neighborhood cafes ignited my passion for the traditional foods of this region.*

1 pound pastured pork, ground, or mild
    Italian sausage without casings
½ pound grass-fed beef, ground
3 ounces jamón serrano, minced, optional
¾ cup grated Manchego or similar cheese
8 garlic cloves, minced
1 tablespoon chopped fresh Italian parsley
2 tablespoons chopped fresh cilantro
2 eggs, beaten
Kosher salt

Black pepper in a mill
2 tablespoons olive oil
1 yellow onion, peeled and grated
1 cup tomato concasse (page 177) or ½ cup
    canned diced tomatoes
1 teaspoon sweet Spanish paprika
1 teaspoon hot Spanish paprika
½ teaspoon ground cinnamon
2 cups green olives, preferably Picholine,
    pitted

Put the pork or Italian sausage, beef, jamón serrano—if using—cheese, garlic, parsley, and cilantro into a medium bowl and mix well. Add the eggs and season generously with salt and several turns of black pepper. Use your hands to knead the mixture until it is smooth and uniform, about 3 minutes.

Refrigerate for 30 minutes.

Use a 1-ounce ice cream scoop to form balls and roll mixture with your hands so that each one is nicely rounded. Set on a sheet pan covered with wax paper.

Set a large, deep sauté pan over medium-high heat, add the olive oil, and when the pan is hot, add several meatballs, being certain not to crowd them. Cook for 45 seconds and then agitate the pan so that the meatballs roll. Continue to cook and shake the pan until the meatballs are evenly browned and beginning to firm up. Transfer the meatballs to a platter and continue until all have been browned.

Reduce the heat to medium, add the onion, season lightly with salt, and cook until fragrant, about 10 minutes. Stir in the tomato, the paprikas, and the cinnamon and add 1 cup water. Stir, taste, and correct for salt.

Return the meatballs to the pan along with the olives, reduce the heat to low, cover the pan, and simmer very gently for about 20 minutes. Remove from the heat and let rest, covered, for 10 minutes.

Serve immediately or cool, refrigerate, and reheat before serving.

Serving Suggestions: With small, roasted new potatoes; with chickpeas; with white beans seasoned with garlic; with grilled bread, for sopping up the delicious juices.

Portuguese Meatballs

Makes about 36 meatballs

   The vinegar in these meatballs makes the flavors soar, just as vinegar is the not-so-secret ingredient that makes chorizo so irresistible.

1 pound grass-fed beef, ground twice
1 pound pastured pork, ground twice
4 ounces Spanish or Portuguese chorizo
      or linguiça, without casings,
      crumbled or minced
1 small yellow onion, grated
6 garlic cloves, minced
1 tablespoon Spanish paprika, sweet, hot, or a
      mix of both

3 tablespoons red wine
2 tablespoons red wine vinegar
Kosher salt
Black pepper in a mill
2 eggs, beaten
6 ounces caul fat, optional
2 tablespoons olive oil, plus more as needed

Put the beef, pork, and sausage into a medium mixing bowl. Add the onion, garlic, paprika, red wine, and vinegar and season generously with salt and several turns of black pepper. Mix thoroughly, add the eggs, and mix again. When the eggs are fully incorporated, use your hands to knead the mixture for 2 or 3 minutes, until very thick and smooth.

Refrigerate, covered, for at least an hour or as long as overnight.

Cover a sheet pan with wax paper.

Use a 1-ounce ice cream scoop to form balls and roll each one in your hand to make it fully round. Set the finished balls on the wax paper.

Wrap each one in caul fat, if you'd like.

Pour the olive oil into a large, heavy skillet set over medium heat and, when the pan is hot, add several balls, cook for 45 seconds, and then agitate the pan so the balls roll. Continue to cook until the balls are evenly browned and are beginning to firm up.

Alternately, bake the meatballs in a 375-degree oven until just cooked through, about 20 to 25 minutes.

To serve as an appetizer, return all the balls to the pan and, with the heat on low and the pan covered, simmer very gently until just firm, about 5 to 7 minutes. Transfer to a wide shallow bowl and serve.

Serving Suggestions: As an appetizer, with grilled bread; in Portuguese Kale Soup (page 129); over Portuguese rice; on sandwiches and in tacos.

Greek Meatballs
with Tomato Lemon Sauce & Tzatziki

Makes about 24 meatballs

A moonlit night, a soft breeze, a carafe of rustic wine, garlicky aromas, the lilt and laughter of voices—this is a Greek feast anywhere in the world and one I have enjoyed on countless occasions. These meatballs are inspired by those balmy nights, when we tucked into avgolemono soup with tiny keftethes, salads of plump ripe tomatoes, lemon cucumbers, slivers of red onion and chunks of tangy feta cheese, lamb-filled dolmades swimming in tomato lemon sauce. I use that same sauce with these meatballs.

1 pound lamb shoulder, ground twice
¾ cup cooked rice
1 small yellow or white onion, grated
3 garlic cloves, minced
3 tablespoons chopped fresh Italian parsley
1 tablespoon chopped fresh oregano
1 tablespoon very thinly sliced mint leaves
½ teaspoon ground cinnamon
Kosher salt
Black pepper in a mill

1 large pastured egg, beaten
Olive oil
Tzatziki (recipe follows)
8 ounces homemade fresh tomato sauce or
    1 7½-ounce can commercial tomato
    sauce, preferably Muir Glen brand
½ cup beef or lamb stock
⅓ cup freshly squeezed lemon juice, plus
    more to taste

Put the lamb into a mixing bowl, add the rice, onion, and garlic and use your hands to mix very thoroughly. Add the parsley, oregano, mint, and cinnamon, season generously with salt and pepper, and add the egg. Mix well and then knead for 3 to 4 minutes to create a fairly smooth paste.

Cover and refrigerate for at least 2 hours or as long as 48 hours.

While the meat mixture chills, make the tzatziki.

To finish, cover a sheet pan with wax paper.

Use a 1-inch ice cream scoop to form balls and set each one on the wax paper.

Pour a thin coating of olive oil into a heavy skillet set over medium-high heat. Add a few of the meatballs, being certain not to crowd them, and then cook for about 45 seconds. Agitate the pan so that the meatballs roll and continue cooking until they are evenly browned all over and have firmed up slightly. Set on absorbent paper and continue until all meatballs have been cooked.

Pour the tomato sauce into the pan, add the stock and the lemon juice, stir, and return the meatballs to the skillet. Cover and cook for 3 to 4 minutes, until the meatballs are cooked through.

Transfer to individual bowls or a serving platter and serve immediately, with the tzatziki alongside.

Variations:
Use all beef or a combination of beef and pork in place of the lamb.
Stuff each meatball with a small (⅓- to ½-inch) piece of feta cheese; chill for at least 30 minutes before cooking.

Tzatziki
Makes about 1½ cups

1 cucumber peeled, seeded, and minced   4 garlic cloves, crushed and minced
Kosher salt   1¼ cups plain whole milk yogurt

Put the cucumber in a medium bowl, toss with about a teaspoon of kosher salt, and transfer to a colander or a strainer lined with cheesecloth and let drain for 20 minutes.

Lift the cheesecloth and turn it tightly to squeeze out excess moisture; return the cucumbers to the bowl, and stir in the garlic and yogurt. Taste and correct for salt.

Cover and chill for at least 30 minutes before serving.

Serving Suggestions: As part of a Greek appetizer or dinner buffet; in fresh tomato soup; in pita sandwiches.

Lamb & Chard Caillettes

Serves 4 to 6

Caillettes hail from France, specifically the south of France, where they date back to the sixteenth century. There are regional differences—in the department of Ardeche, for example, you may find chestnuts included—and regional celebrations, including the World Championship of Caillettes, launched in the town of St. Peray in 2012.

Caillettes are sometimes described as sausages and sometimes described as giant meatballs; it all depends on their shape. They are typically made with pork, pork liver, and a large quantity of chard, spinach, cabbage, or other greens. My version here is inspired by the traditional caillettes but calls for lamb instead of pork. You may use pork if you prefer and you may omit the lamb tongue if it is hard to find, as it likely will be unless you live in an area where lamb is raised, as I do. Caillettes are typically served with a green salad alongside, which acts as a palate cleanser and counterpoint to the rich meat.

1 large bunch Swiss chard, large stems and
    veins separated from the leaves
3 tablespoons homemade lard or olive oil
2 shallots, minced
3 garlic cloves, minced
Kosher salt
Black pepper in a mill
8 ounces young spinach leaves

½ cup chopped fresh Italian parsley
2 teaspoons fresh thyme
1½ pounds leg of lamb, ground
3 to 4 lamb tongues, poached, peeled and
    ground
4 ounces lamb liver or chicken liver, chopped
½ teaspoon ground cardamom
6 to 8 ounces caul fat

Preheat the oven to 350 degrees.

Stack the chard leaves and cut them into thin crosswise ribbons, working in batches, and set them aside.

Cut the stems and veins into very small dice.

Put the lard or olive oil into a large sauté pan set over medium-low heat, add the diced stems and veins and the shallots, and sauté tender, about 7 or 8 minutes; add the garlic and sauté 1 minute longer.

Season with salt and pepper.

Add the sliced chard and ½ cup water, increase the heat to medium, and use a large wooden spoon or spatula to turn the leaves until they just begin to wilt. Cook until the chard is tender, about 5 to 6 minutes. Add the spinach, cover the pan, cook for 2 minutes, uncover and cook until the pan is dry; do not let the greens burn.

Remove from the heat, add the parsley and thyme, stir, and set aside to cool.

Put the lamb, lamb tongue, and liver into a mixing bowl, add the cardamom and season with salt and pepper. Mix well.

Add the cooled chard mixture to the meat and mix thoroughly.

Spread a sheet of wax paper on a clean surface and use a 2-ounce ice cream scoop to form balls, setting each ball on the wax paper as you work.

Spread the caul fat on a clean work surface and wrap each caillette, overlapping the edges.

Set the caillettes, seam-side down, in a heavy pan or other oven-proof container that will hold them comfortably without squeezing them together. A large cast-iron skillet works well.

Set on the middle rack of the oven and bake for 20 minutes or until somewhat firm when pressed with your thumb; do not let them become all the way firm or they will be overdone and, possibly, dry.

Remove from the oven, cover lightly with aluminum foil, and let rest for about 10 minutes before serving.

> *Variation:* Use Lacinato kale instead of the chard and spinach. To do so, trim and discard the tough stems of the kale, slice it very thin, and cook as described (above) until it is completely tender. Remove it from the heat and let cool. Chop the cooked kale before adding it to the meat mixture.

> *Serving Suggestions:* As a main course, with scalloped potatoes and a big green salad; on sandwiches (sliced).

Venison Crepinettes

Makes about 24 crepinettes

The first crepinette I ever tasted was made with fresh venison and it was extraordinarily delicious. If you don't have venison, you can make these with wild boar, buffalo, grass-fed beef, lamb, or goat. Be sure not to overcook the crepinettes, as they will lose that yummy succulence. They are best cooked to rare or medium rare.

3 pounds venison neck, shoulder, or brisket, ground twice

2 tablespoons kosher salt

2 tablespoons minced fresh sage

2 teaspoons freshly ground black pepper

2 teaspoons freshly ground white pepper

1 teaspoon ground clove

1 teaspoon ground allspice

1 teaspoon ground juniper berry

1 teaspoon freshly grated nutmeg

8 ounces caul fat

Put the ground venison into a large bowl, add the salt, sage, peppers, clove, allspice, juniper berry, and nutmeg and mix thoroughly.

Cover a baking sheet with wax paper.

Use a 2-ounce ice cream scoop to divide the mixture into balls and set each one on the wax paper.

Spread the caul fat on a clean work surface and wrap each portion of venison, being sure to overlap the edges as the caul fat will shrink a bit. Press down very gently on each crepinette to flatten it just a bit.

At this point, you can freeze some or all of the crepinettes. To do so, simply set the baking sheet in the freezer for 2 to 3 hours. Remove the frozen crepinettes and pack them into freezer bags.

To cook the crepinettes, set a large, heavy skillet over medium heat and add the crepinettes, seam-side down. Cook for 6 to 7 minutes, turn and cook for another 3 to 4 minutes or a little longer. They should have firmed up a bit but not completely.

Transfer to a platter or individual plates and serve hot, with a simple green salad alongside.

Serving Suggestions: On sliders; as a main course, with mashed potatoes and green salad alongside; in Summertime Spaghetti & Meatballs (page 167).

To drink: When enjoying crepinettes on their own, a medium-bodied red wine, such as a Cote du Rhone or Rhone-style, is ideal. With sliders, pilsner, IPA (India Pale Ale), or iced tea is best.

Lemon Lamb Meatballs

Makes about 20 meatballs

The alchemy of lemon, garlic, fresh rosemary and lamb is absolutely irresistible, including in these succulent meatballs. I like to add sheep milk cheese, which contributes a deep yet subtle resonance. It is not essential—these meatballs are yummy with almost any good cheese—but it is worth the effort it takes to find it, especially if you live in a part of the country where both lamb and sheep milk cheese is plentiful.

¾ cup cooked white rice
½ cup dry white wine, dry hard cider,
   or water
4 or 5 garlic cloves, crushed and minced
½ teaspoon minced fresh rosemary needles
Grated zest of 1 lemon
2 tablespoons freshly squeezed lemon juice
Kosher salt
Black pepper in a mill

1 pound lamb shoulder or leg, freshly ground
3 to 4 ounces Bellwether Pepato, Pecorino
   Fresca, or similar sheep milk cheese,
   grated on the large blade of a box grater
1 large egg, beaten
¼ cup chopped fresh Italian parsley
4 ounces caul fat
1 bunch Italian parsley or several sprigs of
   rosemary

Put the rice in a small saucepan, add the wine, cider, or water and set over low heat. Heat through and mash the rice with a fork to make a slurry. Add the garlic, rosemary, lemon zest, and lemon juice, season with salt and pepper, and remove from the heat. Let cool to room temperature.

Put the ground lamb into a mixing bowl, add the cooled slurry and the cheese and mix thoroughly. Add the egg, mix again, and fold in the parsley. Season again with salt and pepper.

Cover and refrigerate for at least 1 hour or as long as overnight.

To finish the meatballs, cover a baking sheet with a sheet of wax paper.

Use a ¾-ounce ice cream scoop or melon baller to form balls, setting each one on the wax paper.

Stretch the caul fat over a clean work surface and wrap each ball, setting it seam-side down on the wax paper when done.

To cook, set a heavy skillet over medium-high heat, add several balls, and cook for about 45 seconds. Agitate the pan and continue to cook until the balls are evenly browned. Lower

Lemon Lamb Meatballs

the heat, cover the pan, and cook another 3 to 4 minutes, until the balls have just firmed up. Remove from the heat.

Spread the parsley or rosemary on a platter, set the meatballs on top, and serve immediately as an appetizer or use in another recipe.

Serving Suggestions: In soups, on sandwiches, with risotto, over pasta, with Summer Tomato Sauce (page 179).

Fresh Herb Meatballs
with Fried Padrons & Aioli

Serves 4 to 6

When using fresh herbs, it is best to focus on what is in season now, which in turn is easiest to do when you have an herb garden or shop at a local farmers' market. Some herbs, like Italian parsley and oregano, are available year-round unless you live in a particularly cold part of the country. Others, like basil and chervil, are seasonal creatures. Additionally, some herbs, again like basil, are best left uncooked. What I recommend is to use a foundation of Italian parsley and then add other herbs that resonate with the season, like sage in the fall, for example, and tarragon in late spring and early summer. These meatballs are for your summer pleasure, when Padron and Shishito chiles are in season.

Aioli (recipe follows)
2 garlic cloves, crushed
Kosher salt
2 teaspoons coriander seed
¾ pound grass-fed beef, in chunks
¾ pound grass-fed lamb, in chunks
3 tablespoons chopped fresh Italian parsley
2 tablespoons chopped fresh oregano
1 tablespoon chopped fresh thyme leaves
1 teaspoon minced rosemary needles

1 large pastured egg, beaten
1 pastured egg yolk
Black pepper in a mill
4 ounces caul fat, optional
2 tablespoons olive oil
8 ounces Padron or Shishito chiles, or a
    combination of the two
Maldon Salt Flakes or Kosher Salt
½ lemon, cut into thin wedges

Make the aioli, cover and refrigerate it.

Put the garlic into a suribachi (a large mortar), add a few pinches of salt and use the pestle to grind it to a paste. Add the coriander, crush it well and mix thoroughly with the garlic. Set aside.

Put the beef, lamb, parsley, oregano, thyme, and rosemary in a large bowl and toss together. Pass through a hand-cranked or electric grinder, using the smallest blade.

With the mixture in a large mixing bowl, add the garlic paste, the egg and the egg yolk and mix thoroughly. Season with salt, add several turns of black pepper and mix again until smooth and homogenous. Cover and refrigerate at least 1 hour or as long as overnight.

To finish the meatballs, cover a baking sheet with a sheet of wax paper. Use a ¾-ounce melon baller or ice cream scoop to form balls and set the finished balls on the wax paper.

Wrap each ball in caul fat, if you like; if not, leave nude. Preheat the oven to 300 degrees.

To cook, set a heavy sauté pan or skillet over medium-high heat and when it is hot, add as many balls as you can without crowding them. Cook for 45 to 60 seconds and then agitate the pan so that the balls roll. Continue cooking and rolling until the balls are evenly browned and have firmed up.

Transfer cooked balls to the baking sheet and set in the oven.

Wipe the skillet clean and set over high heat.

Working quickly, put the chiles into a large bowl, add the olive oil and toss to coat them. Put the chiles into the hot pan and fry, turning a time or two, until the skins begin to scorch and the chiles soften a bit. Return to the bowl and sprinkle with salt.

To serve, tip the chiles onto a serving board or large flat platter, add the meatballs, set the aioli and the lemon wedges alongside and serve immediately.

Serving Suggestion: To make a meal of these balls and chiles, add some sliced cured meat, such as Spanish-style chorizo or jamón serrano, some grilled bread rubbed with garlic and some small tomatoes cut in half through their equators. Guests rub the flesh of the tomato into the grilled bread and sprinkle with a bit of salt. Start the meal with an avocado gazpacho and conclude with a simple dessert of fresh fruit.

To drink: Vinho Verde, Spanish Cava, or Sparkling Wine.

Aioli
Makes about ¾ cup

3 to 5 garlic cloves, peeled and crushed
Kosher salt
1 large egg yolk from a backyard chicken

⅔ to ¾ cup extra-virgin olive oil
1 teaspoon fresh lemon juice
Pinch of cayenne

Put the crushed garlic into a suribachi or other medium-sized mortar, sprinkle with salt and use a wooden pestle to crush and ground it into a smooth, nearly liquid paste. Add the egg yolk and continue to mix until smooth. Use a small rubber spatula to remove the egg yolk and garlic from the pestle; set the pestle aside. Using a sturdy balloon whisk, begin to add olive oil a few drops at a time, whisking thoroughly after each addition. Gradually increase the amount of oil added to about a teaspoon and continue mixing until no more oil goes into the emulsion; exactly how much oil you use will be determined by the size of the egg.

At this point, the aioli should be quite stiff.

Taste for salt and if it is a bit bland, add a few sprinkles of salt along with the cayenne in one spot and drizzle the lemon juice over it so that it dissolves. Whisk thoroughly to distribute evenly. Transfer to a small bowl, cover and refrigerate until ready to use. During this time, the heat of the garlic will diminish, creating a balanced sauce.

Mexican Albondigas

Makes about 24 meatballs

Living as I do in California, Mexican cuisine is as familiar to me, or nearly so, as the wine-country cooking that comes naturally here in Sonoma County. The authentic flavors of every region of our neighbor to the south are represented throughout the state, in cafes and taquerias, taco trucks, restaurants, Latino markets, and on what I call "the tamale circuit," a word-of-mouth trail that will lead you, after just a few inquiries, to someone who makes the finest tamales in town. My comfort food of choice is Mexican, and barely a day passes that I don't have a taco, quesadilla, tamale, or enchilada. Mexican soups and stews, especially posole, are among my all-time favorites and I've worked for years to perfect my versions, one of which is included in chapter 4.

2 tablespoons olive oil, plus more for frying
1 small white onion, minced
1 medium zucchini, trimmed and cut into small dice
3 garlic cloves, minced
Kosher salt
Black pepper in a mill
½ teaspoon cumin seed, lightly toasted and crushed
½ teaspoon dried Mexican oregano
¾ teaspoon crushed red pepper, ground serrano, or chipotle powder

¾ pound grass-fed beef, ground
¾ pound pastured pork butt or shoulder, ground
1 cup steamed quinoa (page 182), optional
2 pastured eggs, beaten
¾ cup Mexican crema or sour cream, for dipping
1 serrano, minced
3 tablespoons chopped cilantro
1 bunch cilantro, rinsed and dried
½ lime, cut into very small wedges

Put 2 tablespoons of olive oil into a small sauté pan set over medium heat, add the onion and sauté until it begins to soften, about 5 or 6 minutes. Do not let it brown. Add the zucchini, cook for about 5 minutes until it loses its raw look, add the garlic, cook for 1 minute more, and season with salt and pepper. Stir in the cumin, oregano, and crushed red pepper, serrano, or chipotle powder.

Remove from the heat and set aside to cool.

Put the meat into a mixing bowl, add the quinoa, if using, and the cooled onion and spice mixture. Mix well. Add the eggs and mix again; it should be uniform but a tad chunky.

Refrigerate for 1 hour.

Cover a baking sheet with wax paper.

Use a 1-ounce ice cream scoop to form balls and set balls on the wax paper.

Set a large sauté pan over medium heat, add olive oil and, when it is hot, add some of the meatballs, being certain not to crowd the pan. Fry for about 45 seconds and then agitate the pan so the meatballs roll. Continue cooking in this fashion, agitating the pan every now and then, until the meatballs are evenly browned and beginning to firm up. Return the cooked meatballs to the wax paper and, when all of the meatballs have been cooked, return them to the pan, reduce the heat to low, cover, and cook for 3 to 4 minutes, until just cooked through.

While the meatballs finish cooking, put the crema or sour cream into a small bowl, add the serrano and chopped cilantro, season with salt, and stir.

Spread the cilantro over a platter and put the cooked meatballs on top, leaving a space for the crema. Scatter the lime wedges over the meatballs and serve immediately, as an appetizer.

> ***Serving suggestions:*** In soups, including posole rojo (page 127); with queso fundido (page 117); in sandwiches, tortas, and tacos.

Chorizo Meatballs

Serves 4 to 6

 Chorizo, most familiar to Americans as sausage, is not a single thing but rather a category that consists primarily of sausages with distinctive seasonings, especially paprika, cumin, garlic and either white wine or vinegar. Although chorizo originated in the Iberian Peninsula, countries around the world have traditional versions. Many types are fermented and aged, some contain fresh herbs and leafy greens, and a few are simple bulk mixtures that can be used to make delicious Mexican-style meatballs. If you don't have a market that sells bulk chorizo, it is easy to make your own.

Olive oil
1 small yellow onion, cut into small dice
5 garlic cloves, minced
1 or 2 serranos, minced
Kosher salt
Black pepper in a mill
¾ teaspoon chipotle powder

¾ pound fresh bulk chorizo (see *Note*)
½ pound freshly ground pork
½ cup fresh bread crumbs, preferably
 homemade
1 egg, beaten
All-purpose flour

Preheat the oven to 350 degrees.

Pour a little olive oil into a small sauté pan, add the onion, and sauté until limp and fragrant, about 10 to 12 minutes. Add the garlic and serranos and sauté 2 minutes more. Season with salt and several turns of black pepper. Stir in the chipotle powder, remove from the heat, and cool slightly.

Put the chorizo and pork into a medium mixing bowl, add the onion mixture and the bread crumbs, and mix thoroughly. Mix in the egg.

Use a small ice cream scoop to shape the mixture into balls; set the formed balls onto a sheet of wax paper.

Pour about a cup of flour into a wide bowl, season with salt and pepper, and coat the meatballs by dropping them, a few at a time, into the flour and agitating the bowl until they are evenly coated. Return the floured meatballs to the wax paper.

Set a nonstick frying pan over medium heat and, when it is hot, brown the meatballs all over, working in batches; transfer the browned meatballs to a rimmed baking sheet.

When all the meatballs have been browned, transfer them to the oven and cook for 20 minutes. Remove from the oven and keep hot until ready to serve.

Note:
I do not recommend using commercial Mexican chorizo, as it is almost always much too greasy. If you have a good butcher shop near you, ask if they make their own. If not, it is not difficult to do it yourself.

Serving Suggestions: As an appetizer on a bed of fresh cilantro, with Mexican Crema for dipping; in soups; in tacos; in sopas.

To drink: Tequila; Margarita; Mexican beer, such as Bohemia; iced hibiscus (Jamaica) tea.

Homemade Chorizo

To make Mexican style chorizo at home, grind 1½ pounds heavily marbled pork butt or shoulder, put it into a mixing bowl and set it aside. Crush 5 or 6 large garlic cloves in a suribachi and pound them into a paste. Season with about 2 teaspoons of kosher salt and add 2 tablespoons ground ancho chiles, 1 tablespoon sweet paprika and 1 teaspoon each of hot paprika, smoked paprika, ground cumin, dried Mexican oregano and freshly ground black pepper. Add ½ teaspoon each of ground coriander and ground cinnamon. Stir well, add it to the pork and use your hands to mix thoroughly. Add 4 tablespoons best-quality red wine vinegar or organic apple cider vinegar and mix again. Cover tightly and refrigerate for at least 8 hours before using. The mixture will keep in the refrigerator for 3 to 4 days and in the freezer for 3 to 4 months.

Firebombs
Spicy Meatballs with Habanero Hot Sauce & Mexican Crema

Makes about 24 meatballs

These little meatballs can be so hot that they warrant their lighthearted moniker, Firebombs, yet sometimes they aren't. The variable is the chiles, which can range from almost bland to scaldingly hot; it depends on the soil in which they are grown, the weather, the climate and the seed itself. I've made salsas that have taken 5 or 6 serranos and still had very little heat and I've had jalapeños that could peel off your skin with a single touch. You'll need to taste and possibly add more chiles to reach the desired level of heat. For the best results, you also need to grind the ingredients yourself and then let them rest in the refrigerator for several hours, so the flavors blossom and mingle.

¾ pound grass-fed beef, such as top round, in chunks
¾ pound pastured pork shoulder, in chunks
1 small yellow onion, peeled and cut in chunks
1–3 serranos, stemmed and chopped
1–3 jalapeños, stemmed and chopped
3 garlic cloves, peeled
3 or 4 cilantro roots, washed, peeled and minced, optional
¾ cup steamed white rice
Zest of 1 lime
½ teaspoon crushed red pepper flakes

Black pepper in a mill
Kosher salt
¾ cup (3 ounces) grated Monterey Jack
1 large pastured egg, beaten
6 ounces caul fat, optional
¾ cup Mexican beer
1 cup Mexican crema or crème fraîche
Juice of 1 lime
⅓ cup fresh cilantro leaves, chopped
1 bunch cilantro
Habanero or other commercial hot sauce

Put the beef, pork, onion, serrano, jalapeño, garlic and cilantro roots into a large bowl and use your hands to toss together.

Using a hand-cranked or electric grinder, grind the ingedients, using the smallest blade if there is an option. If there is just one size of blade, pass the ingredients through the grinder a second time.

Add the rice, lime zest, crushed red pepper flakes and several turns of black pepper. Season generously with salt and mix well. Add the cheese and the egg and mix thoroughly, until smooth and homogenous. Cover and refrigerate for at least 3 hours or as long as overnight.

To finish, cover a baking sheet with a sheet of wax paper.

Use a 1- to 1½-inch ice cream scoop to form balls and set the balls on the wax paper. If you prefer them wrapped in caul fat, wrap them as described on page 8.

Set a large sauté pan over medium-high heat and when it is hot add several balls, being certain not to crowd them. Cook for 45 to 60 seconds and then agitate the pan gently so that the balls roll. Continue to cook, agitating now and then, until they are evenly browned and just beginning to firm up. Cook all meatballs this way and place them on the wax paper.

Return all the meatballs to the pan, add the beer, cover the pan and cook for about 7 minutes, shaking the pan now and then, until the balls are just firm. Uncover, cook off any remaining liquid and remove from the heat.

While the meatballs cook, put the crema or crème fraîche into a small bowl, add the lime juice, chopped cilantro and 2 or 3 generous pinches of salt and stir well. Set aside.

To serve, spread the cilantro over a platter and set the bowl of creme in the center. Put the cooked meatballs around the bowl and serve immediately, with the hot sauce alongside.

Variation:
Spicy Sweet: Along with the hot sauce and crema, serve a hot pepper jam alongside for dipping. To gild the lily, so to speak, put about half a cup of hot pepper jam into a sauce pan, add 2 or 3 tablespoons of tequila and stir gently over low heat until heated through. Transfer to a small dish and serve alongside the other condiments.

Serving Suggestions: In tacos, burritos, tortas, and soups; in queso fundido (page 117); with Mexican rice and beans; with scrambled eggs and hot corn tortillas.

To drink: Ice-cold Mexican beer, such as Bohemia; margaritas; watermelon agua fresca.

Korean Meatballs with Korean Barbecue Sauce

Makes about 16 small meatballs

Korean-style beef ribs—thinly sliced, marinated overnight, quickly seared and slathered with sauce—are one of my favorite luau foods and just about every luau I've ever attended has included them. Here, I take inspiration from those ribs in yummy little meatballs, excellent as an appetizer or, over steamed rice, as a main course.

Korean Barbecue Sauce (recipe follows)
1½ pounds beef, preferably boneless rib meat, freshly ground
1 small yellow onion, minced
2 green onions, minced
6 to 8 garlic cloves, minced
1-inch fresh ginger, peeled and grated

1 serrano, minced
1 teaspoon crushed red pepper flakes
4 ounces caul fat
3 to 4 green onions cut in 2-inch lengths and julienned
1 orange, cut into wedges

First, make the sauce (see following page), set 2 tablespoons aside and cover and refrigerate the rest.

Put the beef into a mixing bowl and add the onions, garlic, ginger, and serrano and mix well. Add the crushed red pepper flakes and the reserved 2 tablespoons of the sauce. Mix thoroughly and refrigerate for at least an hour or as long as overnight.

To finish, cover a sheet pan with wax paper.

Spread the caul fat over a clean work surface and wrap each ball, overlapping the edges. Set each ball on the wax paper, seam-side down.

To cook, set a large, heavy skillet over medium-high heat and, when it is hot, add several balls and cook for 45 seconds. Agitate the pan so the balls roll and continue to cook until they are evenly browned and beginning to firm up. Cook all meatballs this way and place them on the wax paper.

To serve immediately, return all the meatballs to the pan, add about half the remaining sauce, set the heat on low, cover the pan, and simmer gently for about 10 minutes.

Transfer the meatballs to a serving platter and put the remaining sauce in a small bowl. Garnish with the julienned green onions and orange wedges and serve immediately.

Korean Barbecue Sauce
Makes 2 cups

1 cup soy sauce, plus more to taste
½ cup palm sugar or granulated sugar, plus more or less to taste
3 garlic cloves, crushed and minced

8 green onions, minced
2 inches fresh ginger, peeled and grated
4 tablespoons toasted sesame oil
2 tablespoons toasted sesame seeds

Pour the soy sauce into a saucepan, add the sugar, set over low heat, and stir until the sugar is dissolved. Taste and correct the sweet-salt balance. Stir in the garlic, onions, ginger, sesame oil, and sesame seeds, remove from the heat and cool. Use immediately or pour into a glass jar, cover, and store in the refrigerator for up to 7 days.

Serving Suggestions: As an appetizer, with sauce alongside for dipping; over steamed rice or rice noodles, with kimchee.

Korean Meatballs with KoreanBarbecue Sauce

Spicy Thai Meatballs with Coconut-Peanut Sauce

Serves 4 to 6

Thai foods offer some of the most vibrant flavors of any of the world's cuisines, with an irresistible union of sour, salty, sweet, and hot flavors punctuated by a bouquet of fresh herbs.

Coconut-Peanut Sauce (recipe follows)
8 ounces freshly ground pork
8 ounces freshly ground beef
6 garlic cloves, minced
¼ cup minced cilantro leaves
1 tablespoon grated fresh ginger
1–2 serranos, minced
3 fresh kaffir lime leaves, shredded as thinly as possible

1 teaspoon grated kaffir lime zest
2 tablespoons Thai fish sauce
2 eggs, beaten
½ cup all-purpose flour or rice flour
Peanut oil for frying
1 or 2 bunches cilantro, for garnish
2 tablespoons fresh mint leaves, cut into thin ribbons

Make the sauce and set it aside.

Combine the pork, beef, garlic, cilantro, ginger, serranos, kaffir lime leaves, and lime zest in a medium bowl. Add the fish sauce and eggs and mix until well combined.

Put the flour in a small bowl and dust your hands with flour. Roll about 2 teaspoons of meat between your palms into 1-inch balls. Drop the meatball into the flour, shake the bowl to coat it thoroughly, then transfer it to a baking sheet or wax paper. Continue until all the meatballs have been formed.

Heat about 2 inches of oil in a wok over medium-high heat until it is very hot but not smoking. Add the meatballs, 3 or 4 at a time, and fry, turning once, until lightly browned; it will take about 8 minutes total cooking time per meatball. Transfer the meatballs to absorbent paper and continue until all the meatballs have been cooked.

To serve, spread cilantro on a platter, arrange the meatballs on top, and scatter the mint ribbons over the meatballs. Reheat the sauce, pour it into a small bowl, and set it on the platter with plenty of toothpicks alongside for spearing the meatballs. Serve immediately.

Coconut-Peanut Sauce
Makes about 1¼ cups

1 14-ounce can coconut milk
2 serranos, minced
4 kaffir lime leaves
2 tablespoons minced green onions
4 garlic cloves, minced
2 ounces peanuts, ground to paste

2 tablespoons fish sauce, plus more to taste
1–2 teaspoons sugar
Juice of 1 lime
1 tablespoon minced fresh cilantro
1 tablespoon minced Thai basil

Put the coconut milk into a medium saucepan, add the serranos, kaffir lime leaves, green onions, and garlic and bring to a boil over medium heat. Simmer 2 to 3 minutes. Stir in the peanuts and the fish sauce and add a teaspoon of sugar and the lime juice. Taste and add more fish sauce or the remaining sugar for balance. Simmer 3 to 4 minutes, until the mixture thickens slightly. Stir in the cilantro and the basil and remove from the heat.

Serving Suggestions: As an appetizer; with Green Papaya Salad; in Southeast Asian green curries; over rice vermicelli; on banh mi (Vietnamese sandwiches).

To drink: Pilsner; off-dry Riesling; Thai basil lemonade; young coconut juice.

Pearl Balls

Makes about 12 to 16 balls

I must thank my friend and colleague Chef Colleen McGlynn of DaVero Farm & Winery for introducing me to these delicious morsels, which hail from China. I love the way the sticky rice swells to completely cover the succulent meat inside, so that when you cut or bite into one a symphony of flavors unfolds on your palate. Be sure to use glutinous rice; other varieties will not behave in the same way and you'll be disappointed with the results.

8 ounces glutinous rice
1 pound pork butt or shoulder, ground
2 shallots, minced
2 medium carrots, peeled and grated on the large blade of a box grater
3 garlic cloves, minced
1-inch fresh ginger root, grated
¼ cup peeled and minced cilantro roots, optional

1 tablespoon sushi-quality soy sauce or Thai fish sauce
1 teaspoon kosher salt
White pepper in a mill
1 teaspoon toasted sesame oil
1 egg, beaten
Ginger Dipping Sauce (recipe follows)

Put the rice into a medium bowl and cover with at least 1 inch of water. Cover and refrigerate overnight.

Put the pork, shallots, carrots, garlic, and ginger in a medium bowl and mix well. Add the soy sauce or fish sauce, the salt, and several generous turns of white pepper, along with the sesame oil and egg. Mix thoroughly and refrigerate for at least 1 hour or as long as overnight.

To finish, set wax paper on a baking sheet and use a 1- or 1½- ounce ice cream scoop to form balls. Set each ball on the wax paper.

Tip the rice into a large strainer and shake to remove excess water. Set the strainer over a large bowl to catch the continued drippings.

Pour water into a wok set over a burner so that it comes about a quarter of the way up the side. Set a bamboo steamer rack over the water and have a second bamboo steam rack at the ready. Line both steamers with a sheet of wax paper or parchment and use a knife to make slits in the paper, following the lines of the bamboo, so that steam can enter.

Set one ball at a time into the rice and gently press and turn it so that the grains stick; cover the entire ball. Set each ball in the bamboo racks, leaving at least an inch between each one. When all the balls have been covered, set the second rack on top of the first and turn the heat to high. When steam begins to rise through both steamer racks, reduce the heat to medium, add the lid to the top rack, and steam for 25 minutes. Remove from the heat and let rest for a few minutes.

While the pearl balls steam, make the dipping sauce.

Serve hot, with the dipping sauce alongside.

Ginger Dipping Sauce
Makes about ⅔ cup

3 garlic cloves, pressed
1 tablespoon freshly grated ginger
1 green onion, white and green parts,
   trimmed and minced

½ cup sushi-quality soy sauce
2 teaspoons palm sugar or brown sugar
1 teaspoon toasted sesame oil
½ to 1 teaspoon crushed red pepper

Put the garlic, ginger, green onion, and soy sauce into a bowl, add the sugar, and stir until it is dissolved. Add the sesame oil and the crushed red pepper. Stir again, cover, and set aside until ready to use.

Serving Suggestions: As a solo appetizer or as one of many.

To drink: Iced tea; iced coffee.

Turkish Kofte, with Four Variations

Makes about 24 meatballs

There are so many types of meatballs—kofte—in Turkey that one could write an entire book on just them. Some are simple and mild, as we see in the main recipe; others are boldly flavored and fragrant. Many Turkish meatballs resemble a finger more than an actual ball and are often shaped directly on bamboo or metal skewers and grilled over a live fire, which is an option with these.

2 cups fresh bread, crusts removed, torn into pieces
1 yellow onion, peeled and grated
¾ cup chopped fresh Italian parsley
2 eggs, beaten
Kosher salt
Black pepper in a mill
¾ teaspoon crushed red pepper flakes
¾ pound grass-fed beef, ground twice

¾ pound ground lamb
Olive oil
Whole milk yogurt
Feta cheese
Red onion, very thinly sliced
Cherry tomatoes (quartered) or beefsteak tomatoes (diced)
Hot flatbread, such as pita or lavash

Put the bread into a large mixing bowl, cover with water and let rest about 15 minutes. Press out and pour off the water. Add the onion, parsley, and eggs, season with salt and pepper, add the red pepper flakes, and mix thoroughly for 2 or 3 minutes to soften the onions.

Add the beef and lamb, mix, and then use your hands to knead the mixture for 3 to 4 minutes, until it is very smooth. Cover and refrigerate for at least an hour or as long as overnight.

To finish, cover a baking sheet with wax paper.

Use a 1-ounce ice cream scoop to form balls and set each finished ball on the wax paper. When all the balls have been formed, use the heel of your hand to flatten them just a bit.

To cook, set a large, heavy skillet over medium-high heat, add a little olive oil (enough to generously coat the pan) and, when the pan is hot, add as many meatballs as can fit without crowding. Fry for 3 minutes, turn, and fry for 3 to 4 minutes more. Transfer to absorbent paper to drain and continue until all meatballs have been cooked.

Serve immediately, with condiments on the side.

Variations:

- Add 2 teaspoons Spanish paprika, ¾ teaspoon ground cinnamon, ½ teaspoon ground allspice and several generous gratings of nutmeg to the mixture.

- Use all lamb instead of a mix of lamb and beef.

- Use all lamb, add 3 tablespoons chopped Italian parsley, 3 tablespoons chopped fresh cilantro, and 2 tablespoons chopped fresh mint to the mix.

- Instead of forming meatballs, soak about a dozen bamboo skewers in water for at least 30 minutes. Shape the meat around a skewer so that it resembles a finger about 2½ inches long and an inch across. Cook over a hot grill.

Serving Suggestions: As an appetizer; as a main course with Turkish rice pilaf.

Moroccan Merguez Meatballs

Makes about 32 small meatballs

In Morocco, a meatball is known as kefta and is typically made with beef, lamb, or a combination of the two. Although you do find actual round kefta, it is more typical to find them oblong on skewers. My version here is inspired by both traditional kefta and by the classic Moroccan sausage, merguez.

2 pounds freshly ground lamb
5 large garlic cloves, crushed
Kosher salt
1 shallot, chopped
1 tablespoon cilantro roots, thoroughly
    cleaned
1½ teaspoons coriander seeds
1 teaspoon cumin seeds, lightly toasted
1 teaspoon caraway seeds
2 tablespoons paprika
½ teaspoon ground cinnamon

1 teaspoon crushed red pepper flakes
2 tablespoons minced fresh cilantro
2 tablespoons minced fresh Italian parsley
Caul fat or rice flour
Olive oil, for frying
1 cup whole milk yogurt
1 teaspoon raw tahini
3 or 4 preserved lemon wedges, chopped
1 bunch Italian parsley or cilantro, large stems
    trimmed away

Put the lamb in a mixing bowl.

Put the crushed garlic into a suribachi (a large mortar), sprinkle with salt, and use a wooden pestle to grind the garlic to a paste. Add the shallot and cilantro roots; crush and grind until they are fully incorporated. Add the coriander seeds, cumin seeds, and caraway seeds and grind them thoroughly. Season the paste generously with about 2 teaspoons of salt. Add the paprika, cinnamon, and red pepper flakes and mix well. Fold in the cilantro and parsley.

Add the spice paste to the lamb and mix thoroughly until the paste is evenly distributed and has disappeared into the lamb. To check the seasonings, taste a bit raw or sauté a teaspoon or so until it loses its raw look; correct for salt as needed.

Refrigerate for at least 30 minutes or as long as overnight.

To finish, cover a baking sheet with wax paper.

Use a 1-ounce ice cream scoop to form balls and set each ball on the wax paper.

Spread the caul fat on a clean work surface and wrap each ball, overlapping the edges. Set on the wax paper seam-side down.

Pour a little olive oil into a heavy pan set over medium-high heat and, when the pan is hot, add several of the balls. Cook for 45 seconds, agitate the pan, and continue to cook until the balls are evenly browned all over and just starting to firm up. Set the cooked balls on the wax paper and continue until all have been cooked. Return all the balls to the pan, cover, cook for 2 or 3 minutes, remove from the heat, and let rest, covered, for a few minutes.

Meanwhile, put the yogurt into a small bowl, add the tahini, season with salt, and stir until the tahini is fully incorporated into the yogurt.

To serve as an appetizer, spread the parsley or cilantro over a platter, add the bowl of sauce, and set the meatballs on top. Garnish the sauce with the chopped preserved lemons and serve immediately.

> ***Serving Suggestions:*** As an appetizer; in a Moroccan Tagine (page 143); on flatbread, topped with the yogurt sauce.

Ethiopian Kitfo

Makes about 24 balls

Kitfo is Ethiopia's version of steak tartare and it is absolutely delicious, with a unique flavor and texture contributed by the seasoned butter. It is now common to find kitfo offered cooked in both restaurants and cookbooks, though the traditional dish is raw and that is when it is at its best. Cooking it is, to me anyway, akin to cooking carpaccio, which is, by definition, thinly sliced raw meat—typically beef—or fish.

⅓ cup Spiced Butter (page 174), melted
2 teaspoons berbere (see *Note*)
½ cup minced red onion
2–3 garlic cloves, minced
1 tablespoon freshly grated ginger
1 pound grass-fed top sirloin or beef tenderloin,
    trimmed, minced, and refrigerated

2–3 serranos, stemmed, seeded, and minced
Juice of ½ lemon, plus more to taste
Kosher salt
Black pepper in a mill
1 bunch fresh cilantro, large stems trimmed

First, make the Spiced Butter if you have not already done so and put it into a small saucepan or sauté pan. Add the berbere, set over very low heat, swirl the pan, add the onion, garlic, and ginger, and simmer very gently for 2 minutes. Remove from the heat and cool slightly.

Working quickly, put the beef into a medium mixing bowl, add the serranos and lemon juice, and mix thoroughly. Stir in the butter mixture, taste, and season as needed with salt, pepper, and lemon juice.

Set aside, covered, for 15 minutes so the flavors will blossom.

Spread the cilantro over a platter.

Use a ¾-ounce ice cream scoop or melon baller to form 24 balls.

Set them on the cilantro and serve immediately.

Variation: To serve cooked, form the mixture into 24 balls and press each one to flatten it a bit. Cook on high heat for 2 minutes, turn, and cook for 2 minutes more. Serve hot.

Serving Suggestions: As part of an appetizer buffet with zucchini fritters (page 96), green olives, feta cheese, whole milk yogurt, and Ethiopian or other flatbread.

Vampire Balls

Serves 6 to 10 as an appetizer

Steak tartare—raw beef, cut into tiny pieces or ground, and mixed with seasonings and a raw egg yolk—is a classic French dish, with variations throughout Europe and much of the rest of the world. In the United States, we are often warned not to eat rare, let alone raw, meat. These concerns reflect problems with large-scale factory farms where meat often becomes contaminated. The best defense against such an occurrence is to use meat raised and processed as close to where you live as possible. It is frequently available at farmers' markets. If you can't find local meat, visit a local butcher counter or shop.

1½ pounds grass-fed London broil, trimmed of fat and connective tissue
½ pound grass-fed beef fillet
Kosher salt
Black pepper in a mill
3 garlic cloves, minced
1 shallot, minced

2 serranos, stemmed, seeded, and minced
2 large egg yolks, from pastured hens
2 tablespoons minced fresh cilantro
1 baguette, thinly sliced and toasted until golden brown
Cilantro leaves, for garnish

Using a very sharp knife, cut the beef into ⅛-inch-thick slices; cut each slice into ⅛-inch strips and cut the strips into tiny even cubes.

Transfer the meat to a medium bowl and season with salt and pepper.

Add the garlic, shallot, serranos, and egg yolks and mix thoroughly.

Taste and correct the seasoning. Fold in the minced cilantro.

Chill, covered, for 1 to 2 hours.

Use a small ice cream scoop or a melon baller to make round balls, setting each ball on a baguette slice as you make it.

Garnish each ball with a cilantro leaf and serve immediately.

Variations:

Mustard: Omit the serrano and cilantro. Add 2 teaspoons Dijon mustard and 2 tablespoons minced fresh Italian parsley along with the garlic, shallots, and egg yolks.

Green peppercorns: Use Dijon and parsley instead of serrano and cilantro; add 2 teaspoons brined green peppercorns along with the garlic, shallot, and egg yolk. Garnish with a few more green peppercorns.

Avocado: Cut 1 large or 2 medium avocados into ¼-inch dice and season with salt, pepper, and a generous squeeze of lime juice. Fold gently into the steak along with the cilantro. Serve atop tortilla chips and garnish with tiny lime wedges.

Olive oil: Omit the serrano and cilantro. Use 2 tablespoons minced fresh Italian parsley and 1 tablespoon minced capers (rinsed, if salted). After mounding onto the baguette slices, drizzle a bit of bold-flavored extra-virgin olive oil on top of each portion.

Serving Suggestions: As a solo appetizer, as part of an appetizer buffet, as a first course.

Chicken Kiev Meatballs

Makes about 16 meatballs

These meatballs are inspired by two things, my memory of the Chicken Kiev served at a little French–Algerian bistro where I worked in the early 1980s and, more importantly, by a scene in the first episode of the fourth season of Mad Men, *when a suddenly single Don Draper takes his date to a fancy restaurant that specializes in the dish. Both are fitted with bibs to catch the garlic butter that spurts out when you first cut into the rolled, breaded, and deep-fried chicken breast. I've always thought the dish would be better made with thigh meat, which holds up to lengthy cooking better than chicken breast does. I was right; these little morsels, popped into your mouth whole, are heavenly.*

Roasted Garlic Butter (page 175)
1 pound chicken thigh and/or leg meat,
    ground twice
Kosher salt
Black pepper in a mill
2 tablespoons chopped fresh Italian parsley or
    snipped fresh chives

1 egg, beaten
3–4 ounces caul fat
1 tablespoon olive oil
Fresh pea shoots, small-leaf arugula, or other
    small fresh green

First, make the garlic butter.

After grinding the chicken, put it into a medium mixing bowl and season well with salt and pepper. Add the parsley and the egg and mix thoroughly. Refrigerate the mixture for at least 1 hour.

To fill, set the butter on a clean work surface.

Set the caul fat on another clean work surface and cut it into 16 equal pieces that are as circular as possible (do not worry if they are not even).

Fill a 1-ounce ice cream scoop with the chilled chicken mixture. Working quickly, cut off a nubbin of butter (about ½ teaspoon's worth) and press it into the center of the mixture. Use your fingers to press the chicken mixture around the butter, pinching to seal it.

Set the ball on a piece of caul fat, wrap the fat around the ball securely, and set it on a tray.

When all of the balls are ready, freeze for 30 minutes or refrigerate for up to 3 hours.

To finish the meatballs, set a large, heavy skillet over high heat and add the olive oil. When the pan is hot, lower the heat to medium, add half the meatballs, and cook for 30 seconds. Shake the pan to rotate the balls or, if you are not comfortable shaking the pan, use tongs to turn them. Continue until the balls are evenly browned. Cover and cook for 2 minutes.

While the balls cook, spread the greens over a serving platter.

Put the cooked meatballs on the greens, cover with a sheet of aluminum foil, and cook the remaining balls.

Alternately, serve the meatballs in martini or similar glasses, 2 per serving, with fresh greens in the bottom of the glass.

Serve immediately with toothpicks and napkins.

Variations:
- Instead of roasted garlic butter, use mustard butter (page 175) and serve with ½ cup crème fraîche or sour cream mixed with 1 tablespoon Dijon mustard, for dipping.

- Instead of roasted garlic butter, use olive butter and serve with your favorite tapenade. To make olive butter, combine 1 small minced shallot, 2 tablespoons minced olives of choice, 1 tablespoon minced Italian parsley, and several turns of black pepper with ½ cup butter.

- File this variation under "not for the novice cook." Experienced cooks might want to try wrapping the chicken meatballs in chicken skin instead of caul fat. You'll need a somewhat bigger piece to wrap each ball since the skin shrinks as it cooks. But if you are a confident cook, you can figure it out and I guarantee the results will be delicious. Be sure to season the skin with salt and pepper before cooking and refrigerate the wrapped balls for at least an hour before cooking them.

To drink: A Moscow Mule (vodka, ginger beer, and lime) in a copper mug is the perfect accompaniment. Chardonnay, Dry Rosé, an ice-cold pilsner, and hard cider are also good matches.

Chicken Kiev Meatballs

Duck Meatballs with Sweet Spices

Makes about 20 small meatballs

Duck is increasingly available in the United States, especially in urban areas and at farmers' markets. If you don't have access to duck, consult Resources, page 183. I prefer leg and thigh meat for these delicious meatballs, as it is less expensive than duck breast and lends itself to longer cooking. Do not skimp on the fat or your meatballs will likely be dry; much of the fat is drained off as the meatballs cook, but the lubrication it provides is essential.

1 pound duck meat, skinned,
    in chunks, chilled
½ pound duck fat (the fatty skin of a duck
    breast is best), in chunks, chilled
1 tablespoon olive oil or duck fat
2 shallots, minced
3–4 garlic cloves, minced
½ star anise, lightly toasted and crushed
1 allspice berry, crushed
3 cardamom seeds (not pods), crushed

Kosher salt
White pepper in a mill
¾ cup dry red wine
¾ cup steamed quinoa, preferably red
1 duck egg, beaten
2 teaspoons fresh grated orange zest
Black pepper in a mill
6 ounces caul fat
Olive oil

Connect the grinder attachment fitted with the large blade to a mixer and pass the cold duck meat and fat through it into a medium mixing bowl. Set aside briefly.

Put the olive oil or duck fat into a sauté pan set over medium heat, add the shallots and garlic, and sauté until soft and fragrant, 4 or 6 minutes.

Add the anise, allspice, and cardamom and season generously with salt and white pepper. Increase the heat to high, add the wine, and simmer until it is reduced by half. Remove from the heat, add the quinoa, stir, and set aside to cool.

Add the cooled mixture, along with the egg and orange zest, to the duck. Mix quite thoroughly. Taste, correct for salt, and season generously with black pepper. Chill for at least 30 minutes or as long as overnight.

To finish the meatballs, cover a baking sheet with wax paper.

Use a 1-ounce ice cream scoop to form balls, setting each on the wax paper as you work.

Set the caul fat on a clean work surface and wrap each ball, overlapping the edges and setting them seam-side down on the wax paper.

Set a large, heavy skillet over medium-high heat, add just enough olive oil to coat the bottom of the pan and, when it is hot, add several meatballs. Cook for 45 seconds and then agitate the pan so the balls roll. Continue to cook and agitate until the balls are evenly browned and starting to firm up a bit.

Transfer the cooked meatballs to absorbent paper and continue until all the meatballs have been cooked.

Serving Suggestions: As an appetizer, with Sherry Vinaigrette as a dipping sauce; on a bed of salad greens, with Balsamic Vinaigrette; with mushroom risotto; on sandwiches, with fig and olive spread, olive tapenade, hot pepper jam, or red onion marmalade; in Southeast Asian soups, such as pho.

To drink: Pinot noir from Santa Barbara, Sonoma Coast, or Russian River Valley; Syrah; Rhone and Rhone-style blends.

Turkey Meatballs with Fresh Sage and Cranberry Salsa

Makes about 24 small meatballs

I don't care much for meatballs that call for turkey instead of the meat that is traditionally used, a trend in America because of the perception that turkey is a healthier meat. I think turkey meatballs should celebrate turkey for its own qualities, which means that they should taste like Thanksgiving dinner, which these do.

4 tablespoons butter

1 small yellow onion, cut into very small dice

2 celery stalks, cut into very small dice

¼ cup minced fresh sage leaves

Kosher salt

Black pepper in a mill

Small sage sprig

2 cups, very lightly packed, hand-torn sourdough bread, without crusts

½ cup whole milk or half-and-half

1½ pounds freshly ground turkey thigh

1 egg, beaten

6 ounces caul fat

1 tablespoon olive oil or clarified butter

Melt the butter in a heavy skillet set over medium heat; add the onion and celery, reduce the heat to low and sauté gently until very soft and fragrant, about 15 minutes. Stir in the sage leaves and season generously with salt and pepper.

Put the bread, sage sprig, and milk in a small saucepan set over very low heat. When it is heated through and the milk fully absorbed by the bread, use a fork to mash the bread, reducing it as much as possible to a sort of slurry. Season with salt and pepper, remove from the heat, and set aside.

When the onion mixture and the bread mixture have cooled to room temperature, add them to the turkey and mix thoroughly. Add the egg and mix again.

Cover and refrigerate for at least an hour or as long as overnight.

To finish the meatballs, cover a baking sheet with wax paper.

Spread the caul fat over a clean work surface and wrap each ball, overlapping the edges and setting each wrapped ball seam-side down on the wax paper.

To cook, set a large, heavy sauté pan over medium heat and, when it is hot, add several meatballs. Cook for 45 seconds and then agitate the pan so that the balls roll. Continue to cook until evenly browned and beginning to firm up. Cook the remaining balls.

To finish, return all the balls to the pan, reduce the heat to very low, cover, and cook gently until just done, about 7 minutes more.

Serving Suggestions: As an appetizer, with cranberry relish or cranberry salsa; in turkey soup; on sandwiches with cream cheese and cranberry sauce.

To drink: A pinot noir from the Russian River Valley or Santa Ynez Valley.

Corned Beef Hash Balls with Dijon Mustard

Makes about 16 balls

What is the best part of corned beef hash? It is the crusty little parts when the meat and potatoes have had direct contact with the hot pan in which they are cooked. It is those little morsels that were the inspiration for these meatballs, as there is more surface area for them to become nice and crunchy. The best time to make these is when you have leftover corned beef and cabbage from, say, St. Patrick's Day. I always make more than I need for the main meal, which includes corned beef, cabbage, potatoes, carrots and onions simmered together in one pot. You'll notice I do not include carrots in this meatball recipe; they would contribute a sweetness that I don't want here. If you have a lot of leftover cabbage, use it instead of the fresh cabbage included in this recipe. In a pinch, you can make these with canned corned beef but you'll need to cook the potatoes and onions beforehand.

1½ pounds, approximately, cooked
    corned beef
1 to 1½ cups cooked potatoes
½ cup cooked onion, chopped
2 pastured eggs, beaten
Kosher salt

Black pepper in a mill
2 tablespoons lard or olive oil
4 cups shredded green cabbage
1 cup cooking liquid (from the leftover
    corned beef) or water
Dijon or other mustard of choice

Put the corned beef into a mixing bowl and use a fork to break it up. Add the potatoes, break them up, add the onion and mix thoroughly. Add the eggs, mix well and season with salt and pepper. Cover and refrigerate for at least an hour.

To finish the meatballs, cover a baking sheet with wax paper.

Use a 1-ounce ice cream scoop to form balls and set them on the wax paper.

Set a large sauté pan over medium heat, add the lard or olive oil and when it is hot, add a few meatballs. Cook for 45 seconds and then gently agitate the pan so that the balls roll. Continue to cook, rolling the balls every so often, until they are evenly browned and just beginning to firm up. Return the cooked meatballs to the wax paper and continue until all the meatballs have been cooked.

Put the cabbage in the sauté pan and toss to coat it with the pan drippings. Add the cooking liquid or water, cover and cook until just wilted, about 10 to 12 minutes. Carefully set the meatballs on top of the cabbage, reduce the heat to low, cover and cook for another 10 to 15 minutes, until the cabbage is very limp and the meatballs hot all the way through.

To serve, divide among individual soup plates, add a dollop of mustard alongside and serve immediately.

> *Variation:*
> **With Poached Eggs:** To serve as a breakfast or brunch dish, add a poached egg to each serving, season it with salt and serve with Tabasco or other hot sauce alongside.

> *Serving Suggestions:* Dinner, on a cold rainy night; breakfast or brunch.
>
> *To drink:* Stout; Irish Red Ale; Irish whiskey.

Corned Beef Hash Balls with Dijon Mustard

Dirty Rice Boulettes
with the Devil's Mustard Sauce

Makes about 12 to 16 balls

The best time to make these yummy balls is when you have leftover dirty rice; the full recipe makes between 5 and 6 cups, almost twice as much as what you need for the balls. So enjoy it with fried chicken, grilled sausages, pork chops, or grilled shrimp and save enough to make these. I promise, you will not regret it.

Dirty Rice is one of my favorite Cajun dishes, and I've been cooking it for too many years to count, since long before I enjoyed it in New Orleans, as I now do, whenever I visit. My version is not absolutely traditional, as I don't add the green bell pepper typically a part of this and many other Cajun dishes. I omit it because I find it eclipses other flavors, at least in my own kitchen; maybe you have to actually be Cajun to tame bell peppers.

3 cups Dirty Rice (recipe follows)
2 large pastured eggs
½ cup heavy cream
Tabasco sauce
2 to 3 cups panko

Mild olive oil or other vegetable oil, for
    frying
¾ cup crème fraîche
¼ cup Dijon mustard

Put the dirty rice into a mixing bowl.

Break one of the eggs into a medium bowl, beat it well with a fork, add to the rice and mix well.

Break the remaining egg into the bowl, add the cream and beat together well. Add several generous shakes of Tabasco sauce, mix thoroughly and set aside.

Put the panko into a wide shallow bowl.

Cover a baking sheet with wax paper.

Pour about 2½ to 3 inches of oil into a deep pot and set over medium-high heat until the oil reaches 365 to 370 degrees.

Meanwhile, use a 1- or 1½-ounce ice cream scoop to shape the rice into balls, pressing to compact the rice and set each formed ball on the wax paper.

When all the balls have been shaped, roll each one first in the egg mixture and then in the panko, pressing into the panko to be certain each ball is completely covered.

Using a slotted spoon, lower the rice balls into the oil, one at a time, and waiting for the oil to return to temperature before adding the next ball. Do not overcrowd the pan.

Cook until golden brown all over, turning the balls now and then so that they cook evenly. Use a slotted spoon to transfer the cooked boulettes to absorbent paper to drain. Continue until all have been cooked.

Working quickly, make the dipping sauce. Pour the crème fraîche into a small bowl, add the Dijon mustard and several shakes of Tabasco sauce and stir well. Use as much or as little Tabasco sauce as you like to suit your preference.

Serve hot, with the dipping sauce alongside.

Dirty Rice
Serves 6 to 8

2 teaspoons kosher salt, plus more as needed
1 teaspoon ground cayenne, plus more to taste
1½ teaspoons ground black pepper
1½ teaspoons sweet Spanish paprika
1 teaspoon ground cumin
1 teaspoon dry mustard, such as Colman's
½ teaspoon dried thyme
½ teaspoon dried oregano
½ pound chicken gizzards
2 tablespoons chicken fat, duck fat, lard or mild olive oil

¼ pound ground pork
2 tablespoons butter
1 small white or yellow onion, minced
3 celery stalks, minced
5 garlic cloves, minced
3 cups homemade chicken stock (page 179)
2 bay leaves
1¼ cups long-grain white rice
½ pound chicken livers, ground
2 green onions, trimmed and very thinly sliced

Put the 2 teaspoons of kosher salt, along with the cayenne, black pepper, paprika, cumin, dry mustard, thyme and oregano into a small bowl, stir and set aside.

Dirty Rice Boulettes

Rinse the chicken gizzards, cut them into chunks and either chop them in a food processor fitted with the metal blade or pass them through a hand-operated or electric meat grinder.

Put the 2 tablespoons of fat into a heavy skillet set over medium heat, add the ground gizzards and the pork and cook, stirring frequently, until the meat is browned, about 6 to 7 minutes. Add the butter and when it is melted, stir in the spice mixture and the onion, celery and garlic. Cook over low heat until the vegetables are limp and fragrant, about 8 to 9 minutes. Scrape the bottom of the pan frequently so that the vegetables do not stick.

Add the stock and the bay leaves, increase the heat to medium and simmer for about 8 minutes. Stir in the white rice, cover and cook for 7 minutes. Uncover, stir in the chicken livers, cook for 2 minutes, reduce the heat to very low, cover and let simmer very slowly for 7 minutes more. Turn off the heat and let the rice rest without uncovering it for 10 minutes.

Uncover and use tongs to remove and discard the bay leaves. Fluff with a fork.

Taste and correct for salt and for heat, adding more ground cayenne if you like. Transfer to a serving bowl or platter, sprinkle the green onions over the rice and serve immediately.

Swedish Meatballs

Makes about 30 to 36 meatballs

Swedish meatballs are among the most recognized meatballs in the world, perhaps because they are a popular snack at IKEA, though their fame goes back much earlier, at least to the 1950s and 1960s, when they were a common appetizer in the United States. The meatballs themselves are quite simple; it is the gravy and classic condiment, lingonberry jam, that distinguish them from others. In my version, I use crème fraîche in place of the traditional sour cream to make a more voluptuous but slightly less tangy version. I also use homemade stock. You may use commercial beef broth, though the flavors and texture won't be as good. To serve these meatballs as a main course, add steamed or roasted potatoes, tossed with plenty of good butter, alongside.

for the meatballs

3 tablespoons olive oil
1 yellow onion, diced
Kosher salt
Black pepper in a mill
1 pound ground chuck
1 pound ground pork
1 teaspoon freshly ground nutmeg

½ teaspoon ground allspice
1 cup Panko or coarse homemade
   breadcrumbs (see *Note* below)
2 large egg yolks
2 tablespoons chopped fresh Italian parsley
Lingonberry Jam

for the gravy

3 tablespoons butter
3 tablespoons flour
Kosher salt
Black pepper in a mill

3 cups homemade beef stock (page 181)
¾ cup creme fraiche or sour cream
2 tablespoons chopped fresh Italian parsley

Pour enough olive oil to just coat the bottom of a large heavy sauté pan. Set over medium-low heat and add the onion. Sauté until very soft and fragrant, 15 to 20 minutes; do not let the onion brown. Season lightly with salt and pepper, remove from the heat and let cool.

Put the beef and pork into a mixing bowl, add the nutmeg, allspice, Panko or breadcrumbs, egg yolks, parsley, and cooled onion. Mix well with your hands, a large wooden spoon, or a vegetable masher. Season generously with salt and pepper. Cover and refrigerate for 30 minutes to 1 hour.

Swedish Meatballs

Set a baking sheet or large plate next to a clean work surface. Assemble all the ingredients for the gravy.

Remove the meatball mixture from the refrigerator and shape it into small balls, about 1- to 1¼ -inches. As you work, set each formed meatball on the baking sheet or platter.

Return the sauté pan to medium heat and add the remaining olive oil. When the pan is hot, add some of the meatballs, being careful not to crowd them. Cook the meatballs, carefully turning them frequently so that they keep their shape, until they firm up, about 4 to 5 minutes. Transfer the cooked meatballs back to the sheet pan or plate and continue until all the meatballs have been cooked.

Put the butter into the pan and use a whisk or metal spatula to scrape up bits of meat stuck to the pan. When the butter is foamy, sprinkle in the flour. Stir and cook until it takes on a lightly golden brown hue. Season with salt and pepper and slowly whisk in the beef stock. Simmer gently for 3 to 4 minutes, until the gravy begins to thicken. Stir in the crème fraîcheor sour cream, taste for salt and pepper and stir in the parsley.

Reduce the heat to low, carefully tip the meatballs into the gravy and jostle the pan to arrange them evenly; turn any that are not fully coated with the sauce. Cover the pan and simmer gently for 3 to minutes.

Remove from the heat, keep covered, and let rest for 5 minutes. Transfer to a wide shallow serving bowl and serve right away, with the jam alongside.

> **Note:**
> Panko is a popular brand of Japanese breadcrumbs. If you want to make these meatballs gluten free, check restaurant supply stores near you for the gluten-free version, which comes in 20-pound sacks, perfect for sharing with gluten-free friends.

Scotch Eggs with a Spicy Variation

Serves 4

In the United States, we sometimes see Scotch Eggs in English pubs, but in the United Kingdom, they are ubiquitous, popular for picnics and sold in all manner of shops, from convenience stores to supermarkets. There are many variations of a cooked egg wrapped in ground meat and deep-fried. Fortum& Mason, London's famous department store, is credited with popularizing Scotch Eggs and claims to have invented them, though similar preparations, with different seasonings, of course, have a much longer history in Asia and India. It England, Scotch Eggs are eaten at cold but I think their flavors and textures are best when enjoyed hot.

6 large farm eggs
1 pound freshly ground pastured pork
5 garlic cloves, minced
1 small shallot minced
¼ cup freshly chopped herbs (Italian parsley, chives, sage, oregano, thyme)
1 tablespoon Dijon mustard

Kosher salt
Black pepper in a mill
½ cup all-purpose flour
2 cups Panko
Peanut oil, for frying
Dijon or hot English mustard, for dipping

Set 4 of the eggs in the basket of a steamer and set the basket over simmering water. Steam for 4 minutes for small eggs, 5 minutes for medium eggs, and 6 minutes for large eggs. Let rest in the pot for 2 to 3 minutes, transfer to an ice water bath and let rest for 10 minutes. Crack the eggs on a hard surface, return to the water for 5 minutes, and then peel. Set the peeled eggs on a clean towel and pat dry.

While the eggs cook, prepare the meat mixture. Put the pork, garlic, shallot, herbs, and mustard into a mixing bowl. Add one of the remaining eggs, season generously with salt and pepper, and mix thoroughly.

To assemble the eggs, put the flour in a small and wide shallow bowl. Put the remaining egg into a medium bowl and whisk until smooth. Put the Panko in a slightly larger bowl. Pour about 4 inches of peanut oil into a medium saucepan.

Set a piece of parchment or plastic wrap on a clean work surface and put 1 quarter of the meat mixture in the middle of it. Pat it into a circle that looks like it will wrap around an egg.

Roll 1 egg in the flour, coating it thoroughly. Set the egg in the center of the meat and lift of the sides of the parchment or plastic wrap, pulling it around the egg. Press the meat mixture so that it evenly encases the egg.

Remove the parchment or plastic wrap, gently roll the meat in the egg and then in the Panko, pressing it to coat it thoroughly. Set aside. Continue until all the eggs have been wrapped.

Heat the oil to 360 degrees. Carefully lower 1 or 2 eggs into the oil and cook, turning a few times, until evenly golden brown and crisp, about 7 to 8 minutes. Transfer to absorbent paper and continue until all eggs have been cooked.

Enjoy right away, with mustard or other condiments of choice alongside.

> **Variation:**
> - For spicy Scotch Eggs, add 1 minced serrano along with the garlic and shallots. Omit the mustard and add 2 teaspoons each ground ancho chili powder, hot Spanish paprika, smoked Spanish paprika, and Mexican oregano and ¼ teaspoon each of ground cinnamon, clove, coriander, and cumin. Stir in 3 tablespoons red wine vinegar, mix well, and continue as directed in the main recipe. Serve with Mexican crema alongside.

Heavenly Meatballs

Makes about 36

Anne Jordan, who developed this version of a traditional Middle Eastern meatball, is a writer, author, script doctor, writing and screenwriting instructor, and event organizer with a name close enough to mine that we can be mistaken for each other. We both live in Sonoma County but met only recently, when Anne told me of her plans for a Meatball Festival in Sonoma County in 2018. These meatballs, which are quite easy to make, are perfumed with the spices of the Middle East and spiked with the bright flavor of lemon.

1 cup raw basmati rice
1½ pounds ground lamb
1 pound ground beef
2 pastured eggs, lightly beaten
2 teaspoons kosher salt, plus more to taste
2 teaspoons freshly ground black pepper

3–4 tablespoons Sadaf brand Shwarma seasoning, to taste (see Note below)
2–3 cups beef broth or stock, homemade or commercial
1 lemon, thinly sliced
Tzatziki, page 38, or plain whole milk yogurt, for dipping

Put the rice in a strainer and rinse it several times under cool running water; tip it into a large mixing bowl, cover with warm water and let rest for two hours.

Drain the rice thoroughly. Return the rice to the bowl, add the meat, eggs, salt, and pepper and mix thoroughly. Add the Shwarma seasoning and mix again.

Set a baking sheet or a sheet of wax paper next to a clean work surface. Use a tablespoon to form the mixture into 2-inch balls, setting each one on the sheet pan or wax paper.

When all have been made, set a large sauté pan or heavy cast iron skillet over medium heat and sear the meatballs all over. Reduce the heat to low, carefully pour beef broth into the pan until it barely covers the meatballs. Set the lemon slices on top. Cover and simmer gently for 25 minutes, until the meatballs are cooked through.

Remove from the heat, let rest briefly and use a broad metal spatula or slotted spoon to transfer the meatballs to a serving platter.

Enjoy right away, with tzatziki or yogurt alongside for dipping.

> **Note:**
> Sadaf Shwarma seasoning, which is widely available in markets and online, contains black pepper, chilies, chives, cinnamon, cloves, coriander, cumin, fenugreek, nutmeg, parsley, salt, and turmeric.

Chapter 3

Going Meatless

In this chapter, I touch on the endless possibilities of round morsels made with vegetables, grains and seafood, most of which tend to be called fritters. As I considered recipes—I discarded more than I included—I simply chose my favorites and those closer in spirit to meatballs than not. For example, a chunk of zucchini dipped in batter and deep-fried may be called a fritter but it has little in common with the classic meatball; it is closer to Japanese tempura. But zucchini fritters made of grated zucchini, fresh herbs, spices and eggs have a spirit, an essence, similar to that of the meatball: They are round, with a bit of snap on the outside and tender succulence on the inside.

That said, these recipes and their nearly endless variations should be appreciated for their own qualities and not for the ways in which they resemble actual meatballs. Carrot fritters, for example, are incredibly good, no matter if you are a passionate carnivore, promiscuous omnivore or dedicated herbivore. The ubiquitous croquette, a category so enormous that it warrants its own book, is represented here in a single recipe and one that includes, be forewarned, meat. Still, it belongs in this chapter because meat is not the dominant ingredient. If you want your croquettes without meat, try adding a sea vegetable or seaweed such as wakame in place of the meat.

When it comes to vegetarian foods, I take the natural route, which is to say that I appreciate vegetables for their own qualities and neither use nor recommend meat substitutes. You won't find me making "meatballs" with seitan or soy protein, for example. In the early 1980s, I worked in a tiny cafe that offered soy burgers, which we all hated to cook. They fell apart, messed up the griddle and drove us crazy, all while customers stared to make certain their "garden burger" wasn't touching a part of the grill where meat had been. If only they'd known that Jerome, the owner, had an impish habit of cooking garden burgers where we typically fried bacon they would have been horrified.

"Mmmmmm, this is the best garden burger I've ever had," customers would say when Jerome cooked for them, as we all looked away and tried not to giggle.

Give me real vegetables, please, not fake meat.

I encourage you to experiment, using these recipes as templates. If you have good parsnips—crisp, sweet, not woody—you can make fabulous fritters using the Carrot Fritter recipe or you can make half-and-half fritters, replacing half the carrots with grated parsnips. Sweet Potato Fritters, made of mashed sweet potatoes are delicious, as are fritters made of half mashed potatoes and half mashed celery root.

Most of all, have fun, *have a ball!*

Arancini
Stuffed Risotto Balls

Serves 6 to 8 as an appetizer

If you've ever visited Sicily, you have likely at least seen arancini (or arancine), sold by street vendors in both cities and small towns. Some are filled with peas and ham, some with a thick meat sauce, and some are neat, without filling. Here, I use the little balls of mozzarella known as bocconcini because they are delicious and easy; they require nothing more than to be drained of the whey they come in. This recipe is not at all difficult, but if you are not relaxed and comfortable in the kitchen, you may find it a tad overwhelming. The best time to make it is when you are making risotto. Double the batch and save half for these succulent balls. You needn't use plain risotto either; just about any risotto is delicious as arancini. I'm especially fond of olive risotto filled with tapenade.

Simple Risotto (recipe follows)
3 pastured eggs
4 ounces prosciutto, cut into small dice
Zest of 1 lemon
¼ cup chopped fresh Italian parsley
Pinch of salt

Black pepper in a mill
8 ounces, approximately, bocconccini
   (small mozzarella balls)
3 cups fresh bread crumbs, lightly toasted
Olive oil, for deep frying

Make the risotto at least 2 hours before you want to make the arancini; it can be made several hours or even a day in advance.

Put the cooled risotto in a mixing bowl.

Crack one of the eggs into a small bowl, beat it well, and tip it into the risotto; mix thoroughly.

Put the prosciutto, lemon zest, and parsley into a bowl, add a pinch of salt and several turns of black pepper, and toss together thoroughly.

Drain the boconccini and set in a small bowl.

Line a baking sheet with parchment or wax paper.

Use a scoop—a #18 ice cream scoop is perfect—to gather a ball of risotto and set it in the palm of your hand. Make an indentation in the center, add a bit of the prosciutto mixture, and press in a boconccini. Fold your hands around the rice to make a round ball that completely covers the filling. Set on the baking sheet and continue until all have been made.

Crack the remaining eggs into a small but wide bowl and beat well.

Put the bread crumbs in a second bowl.

Dip a rice ball in the egg, turning it to coat evenly, and then turn it in the bread crumbs until there is an even layer. Set the ball on the baking sheet and continue until all have been similarly coated.

Refrigerate the balls for 15 to 20 minutes.

Pour about 3 inches of oil into a deep pot and set over medium heat until the oil reaches 365–370 degrees.

Using a slotted spoon, lower the rice balls into the oil, one at a time, waiting a minute or so between each addition so that the oil returns to the proper temperature. Do not overcrowd the pan.

Cook until golden brown all over, turning the arancini now and then so that they cook evenly. Use a slotted spoon to transfer the cooked arancini to absorbent paper to drain. Continue until all have been cooked.

Serve hot, with plenty of napkins alongside.

Simple Risotto
Serves 5 to 6

6–7 cups homemade chicken stock (page 179) (see *Note* below)
3 tablespoons olive oil
4 tablespoons butter
2 shallots, minced
Kosher salt

2 cups Vialone Nano, Carnaroli, or Arborio rice
¾ cup (3 ounces) freshly grated Vella Dry Jack, Estero Gold, or similar grating cheese
3 tablespoons chopped fresh Italian parsley

Bring the stock to a boil in a medium-size saucepan and keep it at a low simmer.

Heat the oil and butter in a large saucepan set over medium-low heat. Add the shallot and sauté until translucent, 4 to 5 minutes. Season with salt. Stir in the rice and cook, stirring all the while, until the grains turn milky white, about 2 to 3 minutes.

Add ⅓ cup of the simmering stock and cook, stirring, until the liquid has been nearly completely absorbed. Continue adding the broth, ⅓ cup at a time, and stirring constantly over medium heat until it has all been absorbed, about 16 to 18 minutes in all. Add the cheese and the parsley, taste, and correct for salt.

Set the risotto aside, covered, to cool for at least 2 hours or cool, cover, and refrigerate overnight.

Note: If you have a highly concentrated stock, use just 2–3 cups and thin it with water.

To drink: A rustic red wine.

Chickpea Balls a.k.a. Falafel

Makes about 16 to 18 small balls

The secret to making good falafel, I believe, is to keep them moist and to not overcook them, lest they be unpleasantly dry. This means soaking the chickpeas in plenty of water and not skimping on the time they soak; 8 hours is essential, 10 is even better. Using very fresh herbs is helpful, too, as they contain more natural moisture than herbs that are past their prime. If your mixture seems suspiciously dry, add 2 or 3 tablespoons of water to the paste before chilling it.

1 cup dried chickpeas, soaked overnight in
    4 cups of water
1 shallot, chopped
2 garlic cloves, crushed and chopped
3 tablespoons chopped fresh Italian parsley
3 tablespoons chopped fresh cilantro
2 tablespoons all-purpose white flour
1 teaspoon kosher salt

1 teaspoon ground turmeric
1 teaspoon ground cumin
½ teaspoon ground coriander
¼ teaspoon ground cardamom
Black pepper in a mill
Mild olive oil, grapeseed oil, or peanut oil for
    deep frying

Drain and rinse the chickpeas and put them into the work bowl of a food processor fitted with its metal blade. Pulse several times to reduce the chickpeas to uniform bits.

Add the shallot, garlic, parsley, and cilantro and pulse several times. Scrape the sides of the work bowl, add the flour, salt, turmeric, cumin, coriander, cardamom, and several very generous turns of black pepper. Pulse several times, until the mixture is reduced nearly to a paste.

Transfer to a bowl, taste, and correct for salt. Cover and refrigerate for 2 hours.

Pour 2 inches of oil into a heavy saucepan and set over high heat. When the temperature reaches about 360 degrees, use a small ice cream scoop to form balls and carefully drop several into the hot oil. Cook until lightly browned on one side, about 2 minutes; turn and cook until evenly browned all over. Transfer the cooked balls to absorbent paper to drain. Serve warm.

Serving Suggestions: As an appetizer, with yogurt-tahini sauce, hummus, or tzatziki (see recipe page 38) for dipping; on salad greens, with yogurt-tahini sauce or lemon vinaigrette; folded into warm pita bread, with shredded lettuce, diced tomatoes, thinly sliced red onions, and yogurt-tahini sauce.

To drink: Freshly made lemonade or limeade; plain (unflavored) kefir; lassi with fresh mint, cilantro, toasted cumin seed, black pepper and kosher salt.

Eggplant Polpettine

Makes about 18 to 22

 These "meatballs" are delicious served neat as an appetizer especially when you have vegetarians at the table. This version comes from Puglia, in the south of Italy, though I've added my own flourish in the form of roasted garlic purée, which adds a foundation of rich, deep flavor. You can serve these meatballs as-is or you can add a sauce for dipping alongside; see the end of the recipe for suggestions.

1 large eggplant, oven-roasted until tender, cooled
1 tablespoon roasted garlic purée (page 176)
2 or 3 garlic cloves, minced
Kosher salt
Black pepper in a mill
1 egg, beaten
1 cup (4 ounces) grated Vella Dry Jack or Parmigiano-Reggiano

1 cup homemade bread crumbs, lightly toasted, plus more as needed
1 cup, lightly packed Italian parsley leaves, chopped
Mild olive oil, for frying
1 bunch Italian parsley, long stems trimmed and discarded

Peel the eggplant, chop its meat, and set it in a colander or strainer to drain for 20 to 30 minutes. Transfer the drained eggplant to the work bowl of a food processor and pulse until chopped quite fine but not fully pulverized.

Transfer to a mixing bowl.

Fold in the roasted garlic purée and the minced garlic, season with salt and pepper, and mix well.

Fold in the egg, mix, add the cheese, and mix thoroughly.

Add two-thirds of the bread crumbs, mix well, and add the remaining bread crumbs. If the mixture seems too loose to form balls, add another ¼ to ⅓ cup bread crumbs. Add the chopped parsley, taste, and correct for salt and pepper.

Pour about ¼ inch of olive oil into a heavy frying pan, set over medium-high heat and, when the oil is hot but not smoking, form a spoonful of the eggplant mixture into a ball and drop it into the oil. Add several more, being certain not to crowd them. Gently rotate the eggplant balls until they are evenly cooked and evenly browned. Transfer to absorbent paper to drain; continue cooking until all the eggplant mixture has been used.

Spread the parsley on a serving plate, set the eggplant polpettine on top, and serve immediately, with or without a sauce or condiment alongside.

Serving Suggestions: With marinara sauce; with black olive tapenade; with a cup of plain whole milk yogurt mixed with a teaspoon of raw tahini, a squeeze of lemon juice, and several turns of black pepper; with fresh chèvre thinned with half-and-half.

To drink: Red wine.

Carrot Fritters

Serves 8

I've made thousands of these fritters throughout the years, as they are surprisingly irresistibly delicious. Although they are typically served as an appetizer, they make a tasty main course, too, when accompanied by a delicate soup and a big green salad.

Peanut oil for deep frying

2 pounds carrots, preferably Nantes variety, peeled and grated on the large blade of a box grater (see *Note* below)

¼ cup chopped fresh cilantro leaves

1 tablespoon grated fresh ginger

2 teaspoons cumin seed, toasted and crushed

4 tablespoons all-purpose flour

2 teaspoons baking powder

1 teaspoon kosher salt

Black pepper in a mill

4 large eggs, preferably pastured, lightly beaten

Honey mustard, honey–ginger mustard, or other sweet–hot condiment

Pour 3 to 4 inches of oil into a deep-frying pan and set over high heat. While the temperature rises to 350 degrees, prepare the batter.

Put the carrots, chopped cilantro, and ginger into a mixing bowl and toss together gently but thoroughly. Put the cumin, flour, baking powder, and salt in a small bowl, add several generous turns of pepper, and mix well. Add the carrot mixture and toss thoroughly. Pour the eggs over the carrot mixture and toss quickly with a fork. Do not overmix.

To make the fritters, use a small (1-ounce) ice cream scoop to shape the fritters and drop them, one by one, into the hot oil. Allow the oil to return to the proper temperature between each addition. Fry each fritter for 1 minute, turn, and fry for 1 minute more; use a slotted spoon to transfer each cooked fritter to absorbent paper to drain.

Serve hot.

Note:
The size of the grated carrots is important in this recipe. If you prefer to grate the carrots in a food processor, use the small blade, not the large one, as the gratings will be too big to cook fully as described here.

Serving Suggestions: As an appetizer, on a bed of fresh cilantro; over fresh salad greens, with a warm honey-pepper vinaigrette; as a side dish, with roasted chicken; atop or alongside carrot risotto.

To drink: Sparkling wine (Cava, Prosecco, Champagne), gewürztraminer, Riesling, unoaked chardonnay, pilsner, wheat beer, unsweetened iced tea.

Zucchini Fritters with Basil & Mint

Serves 3 to 4

Costata Romanesco zucchini is a traditional heirloom variety from Italy that has shown up at farmers' markets throughout the country in the last few years. It is delicious raw and cooked and has the added benefit of maintaining its pleasing texture even under lengthy cooking. It has a delicate nutlike flavor that also stands up to lengthy cooking. It is the best zucchini for these fritters, but if you can't find it, use small zukes that have a greater skin-to-flesh ratio than larger ones; this will help keep the fritters from going mushy.

1 pound zucchini, preferably Romanesco, grated on the large blade of a box grater
Kosher salt
Peanut oil, palm oil, or mild olive oil for deep frying
3–4 garlic cloves, minced
3 tablespoons chopped fresh Italian parsley
2 teaspoons cumin, toasted and crushed

2 tablespoons all-purpose flour
1 teaspoon baking powder
Black pepper in a mill
1 large pastured egg, beaten
Mint sprigs and basil sprigs
Whole milk yogurt, crème fraîche, or chutney

Put the zucchini into a strainer or colander, sprinkle with salt, toss, and let sit for 30 minutes.

Use your hands to press or squeeze out the liquid from the zucchini so that it is fairly dry.

Pour about 3 inches of oil into a heavy saucepan or deep fryer set over a medium burner or flame and heat to 350 degrees.

While the oil heats, put the squeezed zucchini into a bowl and fluff it with a fork.

Add the garlic and parsley and toss.

Put the cumin, flour, and baking powder into a small bowl, season with salt and several generous turns of black pepper, and add to the zucchini mixture. Toss thoroughly, add the egg, and toss again quickly, being certain not to overmix.

Use a 1-ounce ice cream scoop to shape the fritters and drop them, one by one, into the hot oil. Allow the oil to return to 350 degrees before adding another fritter. Fry for 1 minute, turn, and fry for 1 minute more.

Use a slotted spoon to transfer each fritter to an absorbent paper to drain.

Spread the mint or basil over a platter, set the fritters on top, and serve hot, with yogurt, crème fraîche, or chutney alongside for dipping.

Serving Suggestions: As an appetizer, as a side dish, as a vegetarian main course.

To drink: Chardonnay, Pinot Grigio, IPA.

Spaghetti Squash Fritters

Makes about 12 fritters

It is important to cook the spaghetti squash thoroughly before using it in these fritters, which should, when cooked, be tender and almost creamy inside.

Peanut oil, for deep frying
3 cups cooked spaghetti squash
¼ cup chopped fresh Italian parsley or
    cilantro leaves
1 tablespoon grated fresh ginger
1 teaspoon, approximately, freshly grated
    nutmeg
½ teaspoon ground cardamom
½ teaspoon chipotle powder or other ground
    chile, optional

3 tablespoons all-purpose flour
Kosher salt
Black pepper in a mill
1 teaspoon baking powder
3 eggs, lightly beaten
1 bunch Italian parsley or cilantro, rinsed and
    dried
Walnut tapenade, crème fraîche, or whole
    milk yogurt, for dipping

Pour about 3 inches of oil into a Dutch oven or other deep frying pan, set over medium heat, and heat the oil to about 360 degrees. Alternately, heat a commercial fryer according to manufacturer's instruction.

While the oil heats, make the fritter batter. Put the spaghetti squash, parsley or cilantro, and ginger in a medium mixing bowl and toss with two forks until evenly combined.

Put the nutmeg, cardamom, chipotle, and flour in a bowl, mix with a fork, season generously with salt and pepper, add the baking powder and stir again. Add the mixture to the squash mixture and toss together lightly.

When the oil reaches 360 degrees, quickly add the eggs to the squash mixture and stir.

To make the fritters, shape a bit of the batter into a ball using a small 1-ounce ice cream scoop and carefully drop it into the hot oil. Continue adding several balls of batter but be careful not to overcrowd them and be certain the oil temperature does not drop. Cook for about 90 seconds, use a long-handled wooden spoon to turn over the fritters, and cook about 1 minute more, until golden brown.

Using a slotted spoon, transfer the fritters to absorbent paper to drain.

Spread the parsley or cilantro over a platter and set the fritters on top. Serve immediately, neat or with walnut tapenade, crème fraîche, or whole milk yogurt for dipping.

Serving Suggestions: As an appetizer, with hot pepper jam; as a side dish in a Thanksgiving buffet.

To drink: Gewürztraminer, dry Riesling, dry Rosé.

Mashed Potato Fritters

Serves 6 to 8 as an appetizer

Who doesn't love mashed potatoes? I suppose someone, somewhere doesn't, but I've never encountered such a person. Vegans won't, of course, eat these because they do contain animal products, but just about anyone else of any age will gobble them up. When you have leftover mashed potatoes, use them to make these yummy fritters. They make a great appetizer, especially in cold weather.

2 pounds potatoes such as German
  Butterball, Yukon Gold, or Yellow Finn,
  scrubbed and cut into chunks
Kosher salt
¾ cup half-and-half, hot
3 tablespoons butter, at room temperature

Black pepper in a mill
¼ cup snipped fresh chives
2 eggs, beaten
2 cups panko
Mild olive oil or other mildly flavored oil, for
  frying

Put the potatoes into a medium saucepan, cover them with water, and add 1 tablespoon kosher salt. Bring to a boil over high heat, reduce the heat to medium-low, and simmer until the potatoes are tender when pierced with a fork.

Drain thoroughly, return the pan to medium heat, and evaporate whatever liquid is left in the pan so the potatoes are quite dry.

Press the potatoes through a potato ricer or food mill into a medium mixing bowl. Pour in the half-and-half, add the butter, and mix with a wooden spoon until smooth.

Stir in the chives, season with salt and pepper, cover tightly, and refrigerate for several hours or overnight.

To finish the fritters, put the beaten eggs in a wide shallow bowl and the panko in a separate bowl. Season the eggs with salt and pepper.

Cover a baking sheet with wax paper.

Pour about 2½ to 3 inches of oil into a heavy pot set over high and heat until the oil is about 365 degrees.

While waiting for the oil to come to temperature, use a 1½-ounce ice cream scoop to make potato balls. After forming each one, turn it in the egg, coating it evenly, and then in the panko, being sure that it is entirely coated with panko. Set on the wax paper.

Fry a few balls at a time, turning each one a time or two so they brown evenly, until they are all golden brown, about 4 to 5 minutes.

Transfer the cooked fritters to absorbent paper and continue until all have been cooked.

Serve immediately, as an appetizer.

Variations:
Potato Bacon Fritters: Fry 5 or 6 bacon slices until completely crisp, drain on absorbent paper, crumble, and fold into the mashed potatoes when you add the chives.

Stuffed Potato Fritters: Cut about 5 ounces of Italian Fontina into half-inch cubes and add 1 cube to each ball as you form it, pressing the potatoes around it to fully enclose the cheese.

Sweet Potato Fritters: Substitute peeled sweet potatoes cut into chunks for half or all the potatoes. Season generously with black pepper and add several gratings of nutmeg at the same time. Serve with melted butter for dipping.

Serving Suggestions: As an appetizer; as an accompaniment to roasted chicken, fried flat fish such as Petrale sole and sanddabs, or roast beef.

To drink: When served solo as an appetizer, enjoy a dry sparkling wine alongside.

K & L Bistro's Salt Cod Fritters

Makes 24 to 32 fritters

I am lucky to live in Sebastopol, a small town in west Sonoma County, California, where we have a great restaurant right downtown, K & L Bistro. It's a family restaurant, with owners Karen and Lucas Martin sharing chef duties and their two young sons often hanging out. It has become my home away from home and whenever they have salt cod on the menu—usually as fritters or in brandade—I can't and don't resist. They are two of the finest chefs I know, with perfect pitch and flawless skills. Karen shared her recipe for fritters with me for this book, though the Romesco Sauce that accompanies it is my own.

Romesco Sauce (recipe follows)
1 pound salt cod
5 small baking potatoes
3 bay leaves
1 bunch thyme
10 tablespoons olive oil

1 large shallot, chopped
5 or 6 garlic cloves
¾ cup heavy cream
1 cup all-purpose white flour or rice flour
1 or 2 egg whites
2 cups panko

Make the Romesco Sauce and store it in the refrigerator until ready to use.

Put the salt cod into a container, cover with water, and refrigerate overnight, changing the water once after a few hours.

Preheat the oven to 400 degrees, pierce the potatoes with a fork, and set on the middle rack of the oven. Bake until very tender, about 1 hour. Remove from the oven, let cool until easy to handle, break in half, and scoop out the flesh. Discard the skins and set the flesh aside.

Drain the salt cod, put it in a saucepan, add the bay leaves and thyme, cover with water and simmer gently until soft and flaky, about 10 to 15 minutes. Remove from the heat, drain, and discard the bay and thyme.

Put the salt cod into the work bowl of a food processor fitted with its metal blade.

Put the olive oil into a saucepan, add the shallot, garlic, and cream and heat gently until it just reaches a simmer. Pour the mixture into the work bowl and pulse several times, until smooth and uniform.

Transfer the salt cod paste to a mixing bowl, add the potatoes, and mix well with a large fork. Cover and refrigerate for at least 1 hour or as long as overnight.

To finish the fritters, put the flour into a wide, shallow bowl. Put the egg white into a similar bowl, add 2 or 3 tablespoons of water, and stir. Put the panko into a third bowl.

Cover a baking sheet with wax paper.

Pour about 3 inches of oil into a Dutch oven or heavy saucepan and set over medium heat.

Use a 1-ounce ice cream scoop to form balls. As you work, dip each ball first in flour, then in the egg wash, and finally in the panko. Be sure to cloak each one completely before moving on.

When the oil reaches about 360 degrees, carefully drop in a few balls, waiting for the oil to return to temperature between additions. Cook, turning now and then, until golden brown. Use a slotted spoon to transfer each fritter to absorbent paper.

Serve hot, with Romesco sauce for dipping.

Smoky Romesco Sauce
Makes about 2 cups

¼ cup slivered almonds, lightly toasted
2 gypsy peppers or red bell peppers, roasted, peeled, seeded, and chopped
5 garlic cloves
1–2 teaspoons chipotle powder, to taste
1 small (2-inch) tomato, peeled and seeded

2 egg yolks
1¼ cups extra-virgin olive oil
Kosher salt
Black pepper in a mill
¼ cup red wine vinegar, medium acid
2 tablespoons fresh lemon juice

Put the almonds, peppers, and garlic into the work bowl of a food processor fitted with its metal blade and pulse several times to reduce the ingredients nearly to a paste.

Add the tomato and egg and pulse again, until the mixture is smooth and uniform.

With the machine operating continuously, slowly drizzle in half the olive oil. Stop, scrape the sides of the work bowl, season with salt and pepper and, with the machine operating, slowly add the rest of the oil. Add the vinegar and lemon juice and pulse several times.

Transfer to a small bowl or glass jar, taste, and correct for salt and pepper. Cover and chill 1 hour before using. The sauce will keep, properly refrigerated, for about a week.

To drink: Dry sparkling wine.

Spanish Croquettes with Jamón Serrano

Makes about 16 croquettes

    Croquettes are as ubiquitous worldwide as meatballs, or nearly so, and there are just about as many variations, with fillings that range from mashed potatoes to every type of meat, poultry, fish, eggs, vegetables and even fruit. Some are flat, some are oblong but most are round, yummy little balls that you can pop into your mouth and savor in a single bite or two. In Spain, a croqueta is tapa, a term that refers to the tradition of setting a little plate of food on top a glass of sherry to keep flies out. I love these and I am lucky to live where Chef Franco Dunn, who calls himself a sausage anthropologist, makes extraordinary chorizo that he sells under the One World Sausage label at farmers' markets throughout Sonoma County, California. When he's made chorizo—his selections vary week by week—I use them to make these addicting little morsels; when he doesn't, I use jamón serrano, Spain's delicious version of cured ham.

5 tablespoons butter
1 small shallot, minced
5 tablespoons all-purpose flour
½ cup half-and-half
1 cup whole milk
1 teaspoon Spanish paprika, mild or hot
Kosher salt
Black pepper in a mill

6 ounces jamón serrano or Spanish
    chorizo, minced
2 tablespoons chopped fresh Italian parsley
1 egg, separated
1 egg
1 cup homemade bread crumbs or panko
Olive oil or other vegetable oil, for frying

Melt the butter in a medium saucepan set over medium heat, add the shallot and sauté until soft and fragrant; do not let it brown. Sprinkle the flour over the butter and shallot, let cook for 1 minute and then cook 2 minutes more, stirring all the while. Stir in the paprika and season lightly with salt and several turns of black pepper.

Slowly pour in the half-and-half, whisking constantly, following by the milk. Whisk until very smooth, lower the heat and simmer gently for about 3 minutes, until the mixture has thickened.

Remove from the heat, cool slightly and stir in the jamón serrano or chorizo and the parsley. Add the egg yolk and mix well until fully incorporated; be certain the mixture is cooled before adding the yolk, as you do not want it to curdle.

Cover and refrigerate for at least 2 hours or as long as overnight.

To finish the croquettes, cover a baking sheet with wax paper. Put the remaining egg white and the whole egg into a wide shallow bowl and mix well with a fork. Put the bread crumbs or panko into a second wide shallow bowl.

Use two spoons (1 larger, 1 smaller) to form croquettes. With the larger spoon, scoop up about 2 tablespoons of the mixture. Use the second spoon to sort of roll the batter off the spoon into the egg. Turn it in the egg, transfer it to the bowl with the bread crumbs, make certain it is completely covered and set it on the wax paper. When all of the croquettes have been formed, set them in the refrigerator for 30 to 45 minutes.

About 15 minutes before cooking the croquettes, pour 2 inches of oil into a wide saucepan and set over medium-high heat.

Set absorbent paper near the stove.

When the oil reaches about 360 degrees, gently put 4 or 5 croquettes in to cook, making sure the oil returns to temperature between each addition. After about 90 seconds, use a slotted spoon to turn the croquettes. Cook another 90 seconds or until golden brown, lift out and set on the absorbent paper. Continue until all croquettes have been cooked.

Serve hot, solo, or with other appetizers.

To drink: Spanish cava, New World sparkling wine, dry sherry, ice-cold pilsner or sour ale.

Crispy Crab Fritters

Makes 12 to 16 fritters

On the West Coast, we make these fritters, developed by my friend Chef Ray Tang, with the plump legs of Dungeness crab, but you should use whatever crab is available near you. If you can, extract the leg meat from its shell in one piece, so that you'll have big chunks, which look more dramatic and taste better than when the crab is broken into small bits.

Crushed ice
1 cup rice flour
1 cup all-purpose flour
1 teaspoon baking powder
2 teaspoons kosher salt
Black pepper in a mill
12-ounce bottle club soda
Peanut oil or other neutral oil for frying

3–4 parsnips or carrots (about 2 cups), peeled and cut into very thin 3-inch julienne
2 cups julienned Butternut squash
½ cup Italian parsley leaves, chopped
1 cup freshly picked crab leg meat, in large pieces
Lemon wedges

First, make the batter: Put ice in a large bowl, filling it about halfway. Put the flours, baking powder, salt, and several turns of black pepper into a medium bowl. Whisk in the soda water. The batter should be the consistency of thin pancake or crêpe batter; if it seems a bit thick, add water, ¼ cup at a time.

Nestle the bowl with the batter into the ice.

Pour 3 to 4 inches of oil into a heavy deep pot and heat it to 360 degrees, using an instant read thermometer to gauge the heat.

Working quickly, toss the vegetables and parsley together in a medium bowl and season lightly with salt and pepper. Use a 3½-ounce ice cream scoop to pick up some of the vegetables and then tuck 1 or 2 pieces of crab in the center, pressing lightly. Carefully put the mixture into the batter and turn to coat it evenly. Use your fingers to transfer the bundle to the hot oil. Make 2 or 3 more fritters; do not add more as the temperature of the oil will drop.

Fry each fritter for 1½ to 2 minutes, turn and fry until golden brown all over. Use a flat wire strainer to transfer the fritters to a platter covered with absorbent paper to drain. When all the fritters have been made, garnish with lemon wedges and enjoy right away.

Macaroni, Cheese & Bacon Balls

Serves 8 to 10

Taste of Sonoma, which typically takes place in late August, is one of the biggest annual food and wine events in Sonoma County. One of my favorite parts is the Bubble Lounge, a little outdoor area that requires a VIP ticket for admission. There's shade and several stations pairing sparkling wine with a chef's specialty. One year, Gloria Ferrer worked with Feast Catering, which paired their delicious Brut with macaroni and cheese lollipops, a devilishly good indulgence. This is my version.

Macaroni and Cheese with Bacon (recipe follows), well chilled

2 eggs

2 cups Panko or 2 cups coarse-ground homemade breadcrumbs, plus more as needed

3 tablespoons butter

Peanut oil, for deep frying

Round wooden lollipop sticks, 4- to 6-inches long

Make the macaroni and cheese several hours or the day before serving the balls. Chill it thoroughly.

To make the balls, set a sheet pan next to a clean work surface and cover it with a few layers of absorbent paper. Put the eggs into a medium bowl and whisk until very smooth.

Put the butter into a large heavy sauté pan set over medium heat. When the butter is completely melted, add the Panko or breadcrumbs, season with salt and pepper, and toast, stirring gently all the while, until they take on a bit of color, 3 to 4 minutes. Remove from the heat.

Use a 3-ounce ice cream scoop to form balls, setting each one on the baking sheet. When all balls have been formed, dampen your hands and press each one together, so that it is quite compact. Dip the balls, one at a time, first in the egg and then in the bread crumbs, turning them so that they are evenly coated. Set each on back on the sheet pan.

Set the sheet pan with the balls in the freezer.

Pour about 4 inches of oil into a heavy saucepan and heat to 360 degrees.

When the oil reaches the proper temperature, remove the balls from the freezer. Carefully lower 2 or 3 balls into the hot oil, allowing it to return to full temperature between additions. Cook for 2 minutes or so, turn and cook until evenly browned all over. Use a slotted spoon to return each ball to absorbent paper and immediately push a wooden stick into each one.

Continue until all the balls have been cooked.

Enjoy while still warm.

Macaroni and Cheese with Bacon
Serves 4 to 6

Butter, at room temperature
2 teaspoons Colman's dry mustard
2 teaspoons Tabasco sauce
1½ cups heavy cream or unsweetened condensed milk
2 eggs, beaten
1½ pounds cheddar cheese, medium or sharp, grated

3 ounces bacon, cooked until crisp, drained, and crumbled
12 ounces ditalini, cooked al dente, drained, and rinsed
Black pepper in a mill
Kosher salt
1 cup fresh bread crumbs

Preheat the oven to 350 degrees. Butter a large baking dish. In a large bowl, whisk together the mustard and Tabasco sauce until smooth. Let rest 15 to 20 minutes.

Add the cream and the eggs to the bowl, mix thoroughly and stir in about two-thirds of the cheese. Fold in the pasta, add the bacon and the remaining cheese and season generously with black pepper. Season to taste with salt.

Pour the mixture into the baking dish, cover the dish tightly with aluminum foil and bake for 25 minutes. Remove from the oven, let cool and chill for at least 4 hours or as long as overnight.

Vietnamese Shrimp Balls

Makes 18 to 24 balls

These fragrant little morsels are so light, so delicate, that they practically float from the plate into your mouth. Enjoy them as an appetizer or add them to Asian noodle salads such as Vietnamese bün, to congee (also known as jook and rice porridge), and to simple Asian chicken soup, with or without coconut milk.

Sweet and Sour sauce, for dipping (recipe follows)

1½ pounds shrimp, peeled, deveined, and chopped

3 ounces fatty pork shoulder, chopped

3 green onions, white part only, trimmed and cut into very thin slices

2 teaspoons grated fresh ginger

1 tablespoon rice wine or sherry

Pinch of sugar

½ teaspoon kosher salt

¼ teaspoon ground white pepper

2 egg whites

Cornstarch

Peanut oil, for deep frying

1 bunch cilantro, trimmed

Make the sauce and set it aside.

Put the shrimp and pork on a clean work surface and use a Chinese cleaver to mince them until they nearly form a paste. Add the green onion and ginger and continue to mince until almost smooth. (Alternately, put the ingredients into the work bowl of a food processor fitted with a metal blade and pulse several times, until fairly smooth.) Add the wine or sherry, sugar, salt, and pepper, and mix well. Cover and set aside.

Put the egg whites into a deep bowl and use a balloon whisk to whip them until they form soft peaks.

Pour about 3 inches of oil into a heavy saucepan, wok, or deep fryer and heat to 360 degrees.

Working quickly, fold the shrimp mixture into the egg whites; don't overmix.

Put corn starch onto a medium plate.

Set a baking sheet next to a clean work surface and cover it with a few layers of absorbent paper. Use your fingers to form 1-inch balls, set 2 or 3 in the corn starch and agitate the plate to coat the balls thoroughly. Carefully drop several balls into the hot oil and cook for about 6 minutes, turning now and then, until they are golden brown. Use a slotted spoon or wire strainer to transfer the balls to the sheet pan and continue until all have been cooked.

Spread the cilantro over a platter, set the balls on top, enjoy right away, with the sauce, reheated if necessary, alongside.

Sweet and Sour Sauce
Makes about 1 cup

1 tablespoon cornstarch
¼ cup rice vinegar or apple cider vinegar,
    plus more to taste
¼ cup packed brown sugar, plus more to
    taste

¼ cup ketchup
Pinch of salt
1–3 garlic cloves, pressed

Put the cornstarch into a small bowl, add 3 tablespoons water, stir until smooth and set aside.

Put the vinegar and brown sugar into a small saucepan set over very low heat, stir until the sugar dissolves, add the ketchup, salt, and garlic cloves and stir well.

Carefully taste the mixture and adjust for sweet and sour balance.

Add the cornstarch and cook gently until the mixture thickens, 2 or 3 minutes. Remove from the heat and keep warm.

Vietnamese Shrimp Balls

Parsnip Fritters with Horseradish Cream

Serves 4 to 6

In *The Original White House Cookbook (1887; reissued by The Werner Company / Ottenheimer Publishers, 1999)*, a recipe for parsnip fritters, made with cooked and mashed parsnips, are said to have been served at Thanksgiving during Grover Cleveland's presidency. They were very simple, with no seasonings and no condiments. They were more like little parsnip cakes, as they were not deep-fried but, instead, flattened and fried in just a bit of lard. I prefer both the taste and texture of round fritters made with raw parsnips, though you can make the historic version by substituting parsnips for potatoes in the recipe for Mashed Potato Fritters on page 100. Horseradish cream is an ideal counterpoint to the natural sweetness of the parsnips.

Peanut oil for deep frying

1½ pounds parsnips, trimmed and grated on the large blade of a box grater

6 tablespoons minced fresh Italian parsley

3 tablespoons all-purpose flour

1 teaspoon freshly ground nutmeg

½ teaspoon ground coriander seed

Pinch of ground cayenne or other ground chile

1½ teaspoons baking powder

1 teaspoon kosher salt, plus more as needed

Black pepper in a mill

3 pastured eggs, lightly beaten

2 tablespoons peeled and grated horseradish root

½ lemon

¾ cup crème fraiche

Pour 3 to 4 inches of peanut oil into a deep saucepan or deep fryer, set over high heat, and bring the temperature to 360 degrees.

While the oil heats, combine the ingredients. Put the parsnips and ⅔ of the parsley into a mixing bowl and set aside. Put the flour, nutmeg, coriander, cayenne or other chili, baking powder, and 1 teaspoon of salt into a small bowl and mix well. Tip it into the parsnips and use 2 forks to toss together. Add the eggs and mix quickly but thoroughly; do not overmix.

Working quickly, put the grated horseradish into a small bowl, add the juice of the half lemon, season with a few pinches of salt and several turns of black pepper. Stir in the crème fraiche, taste for salt and acid, cover, and set aside.

Use a 1-inch ice cream scoop to shape the fritters and drop them, one by one, into the hot oil. Do not overcrowd them. Cook for about 1 minute, turn and cook for another minute, until golden brown all over.

Transfer to absorbent paper and continue until all fritters have been cooked.

Serve right away, with the horseradish sauce alongside.

Soft-Boiled & Deep-Fried Eggs
with Roasted Asparagus & Lemon Vinaigrette

Serves 4

This dish is inspired by one served at my neighborhood restaurant, K & L Bistro, in the spring, when we have beautiful asparagus. I love to make it when my own tiny asparagus patch sends up its shoots. When asparagus is not in season, serve the eggs over roasted potatoes or sautéed greens.

1 pound spring asparagus, fattest stalks
    available
Olive oil
Kosher salt
1 small shallot, minced
2 tablespoons freshly squeezed lemon juice
5 tablespoons extra virgin olive oil, plus more
    to taste

Black pepper in a mill
4 pastured eggs
Peanut oil or other neutral oil, for frying
2 tablespoons butter, melted
½ cup all-purpose flour
1 cup Panko

Preheat the oven to 475 degrees.

Snap off and discard the tough stalks of the asparagus, put the green spears on a baking sheet and drizzle with just enough olive oil to lubricate the asparagus. Season lightly with salt. Set on the middle rack of the oven and cook until the asparagus is tender, from 7 to 15 minutes, depending on how fat it is. Remove from the oven and set aside briefly.

While the asparagus cooks, put the shallot into a small bowl, add the lemon juice and 2 or 3 very generous pinches of salt. Whisk in the olive oil, taste for salt and acid and add several turns of black pepper. Set aside.

Set 4 of the eggs in a small saucepan, cover with water, bring to a boil over high heat, and simmer for 3 minutes for small and medium eggs and 4 minutes for larger eggs. Transfer to an ice water bath.

When the eggs are cool enough to handle, carefully peel them. If the shell doesn't come off easily, crack each egg all over on a hard surface, return to the ice water bath and let rest for about 15 minutes and then peel.

Set the peeled eggs on a clean towel and pat dry.

Pour about 3 to 4 inches of oil into a deep saucepan or deep fryer and heat to 360 degrees.

Take one of the dried eggs and roll it in the flour, coating it thoroughly, then roll it in the butter. Transfer it to the Panko and press it into the crumbs, turning it so it is evenly coated. Set on a paper towel and continue until all eggs are coated.

Divide the asparagus among individual plates.

Using a wire strainer, lower 1 egg into the hot oil, cook for about 30 seconds, roll the egg and cook for another 30 seconds, until it is golden brown all over. Lift up the egg, let oil drip back into the pan, and set it on top of the asparagus. Continue until all eggs have been cooked.

Drizzle dressing over each portion and serve right away, with salt and pepper alongside for seasoning the egg yolk.

Chapter 4

Context Is Everything

No woman—nor man—lives by meatballs alone. As good as a succulent meatball is neat, without accompaniment, meatballs are typically served in something or with something. Spaghetti and Meatballs. Meatball soup. A meatball sandwich.

In this chapter, I include classics—you'll find a truly exuberant version of spaghetti and meatballs here, a *tour-de-force* from a Sicilian friend—and break out of the box, trampling the boundaries and running with my succulent little meatballs toward my goal, new ways to savor these yummy little morsels. I love meatballs in soups, in salads, folded into tender corn tortillas and slathered in the melted cheese of queso fundido.

Some dishes don't require a recipe. If you love, say, macaroni and cheese—and who doesn't?—add your favorite meatballs. Spaghetti al Pesto? This classic soars with some Fresh Herb Meatballs (page 45) alongside or on top, as do grits, creamy polenta, risotto and potato purée, which is similar to mashed potatoes but with about five times as much butter.

You can add your favorite meatballs to a mixed grill, especially a summertime mixed grill, with corn on the cob among the selections. You can wrap almost any meatball in bacon, thread it onto a skewer and cook it over charcoal or a wood fire. Then, if you're in a mood to show off, slather some good bread with mayonnaise, layer on some sliced tomatoes and set those bacon-wrapped grilled meatballs on top. Add a piece of tender butter lettuce and *Voila!* it's a Meatball BLT.

Queso Fundido with Chorizo Meatballs

Serves 6 to 8

Queso fundido, simply seasoned melted cheese enjoyed with hot corn tortillas or tortilla chips, is beyond delicious. If you serve this before a large meal, everyone will ruin their appetites by overindulging. I've learned that the hard way. A big green salad and maybe a delicate soup is all you need to accompany this.

Chorizo Meatballs, (page 50), hot
1½ pounds Monterey Jack, grated on the large blade of a box grater
½ pound queso cotija or feta, crumbled
4 garlic cloves, minced
2 serranos, minced

1 teaspoon chipotle powder
3 poblanos, roasted, seeded, and cut into thin strips
½ cup chopped fresh cilantro
2–3 dozen small corn tortillas, hot

Make the Chorizo Meatballs and set them aside, covered to keep them warm.

Preheat the oven to 475 degrees.

Put the cheeses, garlic, serranos, and chipotle powder into a bowl and use two forks to toss together until evenly mixed.

Transfer to an earthenware dish, set on the middle rack of the oven, and cook for 12 to 15 minutes, until the cheese is fully melted and bubbly. Scatter the poblano strips over the cheese, set the meatballs on top, and cook for 5 minutes more.

Remove from the oven, set on the table (be sure to protect the table with a folded tea towel), and scatter the cilantro over it.

To enjoy, each guest takes one or two tortillas in one hand, smears cheese over the surface of the top one, and adds a meatball.

To drink: Agua fresca or ice-cold Mexican beer.

White Bean, Garlic & Meatball Soup

Serves 6 to 8

The first time I had this soup—or a soup very much like it—was at a party at my friend L. John Harris's house. John was my first book publisher and editor (and he contributed the foreword to this book), but he is best known, perhaps, for starting the Garlic Revolution back in the mid-1970s, when he wrote The Book of Garlic. *He was also a cofounder of the Gilroy Garlic Festival and a waiter (briefly) at Berkeley's legendary Chez Panisse, where he long had a big table of friends for the restaurant's annual Bastille Day Garlic Festival. On this particular occasion, we were celebrating and honoring filmmaker Les Blank, who joined us, of course. John's beautiful home, in the hills of North Berkeley, has an enormous hearth in its lower garden and I remember sitting there for a long time, mesmerized by a cauldron of soup hanging over the wood fire, so fragrant with garlic's enticing aromas. I watched as little meatballs rose to the surface, sank beneath it, and reappeared, over and over. The soup was just one of many garlicky dishes, many of which I prepared, and after we'd all had our fill, we went into John's study and watched Les's film* Garlic Is As Good As Ten Mothers. *If you've never seen it, you should. Just put the soup on to cook, watch the film, and I guarantee you will be ravenous by the time it ends. This mimics how Les showed the film all over the country and in Europe when it was first released; he and an assistant placed toaster ovens on either side of the screen and roasted garlic as the film played, filling the theater with delicious aromas. At some screenings, a garlicky banquet followed. Les passed away a few years after that wonderful day at John's house and we all miss his quiet, gentle ways, keen eye, and passion for great food.*

1 pound cannellini beans or other white bean, soaked in water for several hours
3 tablespoons olive oil
1 yellow onion, cut into small dice
1 carrot, peeled and minced
1 garlic bulb, cloves separated, peeled, crushed, and minced
Kosher salt
Black pepper in a mill

8 cups chicken or beef stock (pages 179, 181)
½ cup chopped fresh Italian parsley
Roasted Garlic Meatballs, browned (page 27)
1½ cups (6 ounces) grated Parmigiano-Reggiano, Romano-Pecorino, or similar cheese
Best-quality extra-virgin olive oil, optional
Hearth bread, preferably sourdough

Drain and rinse the white beans and set them aside briefly.

Pour the olive oil into a large, heavy soup pot set over medium-low heat, add the onion, and sauté until it is limp and fragrant, about 12 minutes. Add the carrot and continue to cook until it softens, about 6 or 7 minutes more. Add the garlic, stir gently, and cook 1 minute longer. Season generously with salt and several turns of pepper.

Pour in the stock and 4 cups of water, increase the heat to high, and bring the liquid to a boil. Skim off and discard any foam that collects on the liquid. Reduce the heat and simmer gently until the beans are very tender, about 45 to 50 minutes.

Add the parsley, stir, carefully tip in the meatballs, and continue to simmer gently for 20 minutes. Add the cheese, cover the pot, and remove from the heat.

Let rest, covered, for 15 to 30 minutes. Taste and correct for salt and pepper.

Serve immediately or cool completely, refrigerate overnight, and reheat before serving.

To serve immediately, heat the hearth bread and ladle the soup into bowls, soup plates, or large mugs. If using, add a swirl of olive oil to each portion and serve with bread on the side.

John Ash's Chicken & Shrimp Meatball Soup

Serves 6

John Ash, chef, cookbook author, and internationally renowned cooking teacher, is a dear friend and colleague. I contributed a recipe to his most recent book, Culinary Birds: The Ultimate Poultry Cookbook, *which won a James Beard Award in 2014. This recipe, which John shared with me, is adapted from one in his book and is a lovely example of both the soups and the meatballs of Southeast Asia, where meatballs are typically either cooked directly in a simmering liquid or steamed without being sautéed first.*

4 ounces thin rice noodles
½ pound peeled and deveined shrimp
½ pound boneless, skinless chicken thighs
2 teaspoons finely chopped garlic
3 tablespoons finely chopped green onions
    including the green tops
2 tablespoons fish sauce
½ teaspoon freshly ground black pepper
1 teaspoon sugar
8 cups rich chicken stock (page 179)

2 tablespoons soy sauce
1 tablespoon brown sugar
2 teaspoons chili garlic sauce, or to taste
1 2-inch piece fresh ginger, peeled and cut in
    fine julienne
¼ cup fresh lime juice, from 3–4 limes
3 cups gently packed fresh baby spinach
Cilantro sprigs
Fried garlic or shallots, optional

Prepare the noodles according to package directions, drain thoroughly, and set aside.

Put the shrimp and chicken in a food processor fitted with its metal blade and pulse until coarsely chopped. Transfer the mixture to a large bowl, using a rubber spatula to scrape the sides of the food processor's work bowl, and stir in the garlic, green onions, fish sauce, black pepper, and sugar.

Line a baking sheet with wax paper.

Using a tablespoon to measure, gently roll each spoonful into a ball and set on the wax paper.

Pour the stock, soy sauce, brown sugar, chile garlic sauce, and ginger into a medium soup pot set over high heat and bring to a boil. Reduce the heat so that the mixture simmers gently and spoon off any foam that forms on the surface.

Gently drop each meatball into the simmering stock and cook for 6 minutes, or until the meatballs are just cooked through. Keep the soup at a very gentle simmer so it doesn't cloud.

Taste and adjust the seasoning to your preference, adding more fish sauce if it seems a bit flat and more chile garlic sauce for more heat. Divide the noodles, lime juice, and spinach among soup bowls, add the meatballs, and ladle the broth over each portion.

Top with cilantro and fried garlic or shallots, if using.

> ***To drink:*** Thai iced tea; iced Hawaiian coffee; ice-cold Singha (Thai beer).

Chicken Soup with Walnut Balls and Spaghetti Squash

Serves 8

You can use almost any meatball in this yummy soup, but the combination of walnuts and spaghetti squash is delightful, especially in the fall when there's a new walnut crop and spaghetti squash is just coming on. The very best gift you can give any soup is homemade stock. It's not hard to prepare and you can always make a double or triple batch, freeze it in 4-cup portions, and have it on hand whenever you're inspired to make a soup. I do this four times a year and am never without good homemade stock.

1½ cups walnut pieces, minced
½ cup ground walnuts
½ cup (2 ounces) grated Dry Jack,
    Parmigiano-Reggiano, or similar cheese
1 garlic clove, minced
1 small white onion, minced
5 tablespoons minced fresh Italian parsley

3 tablespoons chopped fresh oregano
Kosher salt
Black pepper in a mill
3 eggs, beaten
8 cups homemade chicken stock (page 179)
4 cups cooked spaghetti squash
(see *Note*)

Put the walnuts, ground walnuts, cheese, garlic, onion, 2 tablespoons of the parsley, and 2 tablespoons of the oregano into a medium bowl, season with salt and several turns of black pepper, and mix well. Add the eggs and mix until you have a uniform paste.

Cover a baking sheet with wax paper.

Use a ¾-ounce ice cream scoop or melon baller to shape the mixture into balls; set each ball onto the wax paper as you work. Cover and chill for 30 minutes.

Cook the balls in boiling, salted water for 7 to 8 minutes, until cooked through. Line a sheet pan with absorbent paper and use a slotted spoon to transfer the cooked balls to the paper to drain. Cover with aluminum foil to keep warm. Alternately, you may steam the balls, preferably in a bamboo steamer set over simmering water, for about 8 minutes or until cooked through.

Working quickly, pour the chicken stock into a soup pot and set over medium-high heat. Stir in the spaghetti squash and the remaining parsley and oregano. Taste and correct for salt; season with several turns of pepper.

Divide the meatballs among individual soup plates or bowls and ladle the soup on top. Serve immediately.

> **Note:**
> The easiest way to prepare spaghetti squash is to cut it in half, carefully scoop out the seeds, season with salt and pepper, and bake in a 350-degree oven until it is tender. Remove it from the oven, let it cool, and then use a fork to scrape out the flesh, which will naturally separate into pasta-like strands.

> **To drink:** A chilled pilsner; Riesling; iced tea.

Sopa de Fideo y Albondigas

Serves 6 to 8

This soup is inspired by the fideos of Barcelona, a dish in which short noodles, about 1-inch long, are prepared similarly to paella. It can be simple, with just the dark toasted pasta simmered in a fish stock and served with a big dollop of allioli, or complex, with a cornucopia of fish, meats, and vegetables. Here, the pasta is toasted and then incorporated into a tangy soup with spicy meatballs. Most Latin markets sell fideo in 8-ounce packages. It is usually offered in a variety of widths; I recommend the thinnest for this soup. If you can't find it, you can use coiled angel hair pasta and simply break it into short pieces.

Chorizo Meatballs (page 50)
4 tablespoons chicken fat or olive oil
8 ounces fideo or angel hair pasta, broken
    into 1-inch pieces
1 yellow onion, minced
2–3 serranos, seeded and minced
4 garlic cloves, minced
Kosher salt
Black pepper in a mill

1 28-ounce can crushed tomatoes
8 cups homemade chicken stock (page 179)
1 tablespoon minced fresh cilantro
2 tablespoons minced fresh Italian parsley
Juice of 1 lime
2 cups (8 ounces) grated Jack cheese
Hot corn tortillas
Lime wedges

Make the meatballs and set them aside.

Heat the fat or olive oil in a large, deep skillet or heavy saucepan set over medium-low heat, add the pasta, and fry until it is deep golden brown, stirring continuously and taking care not to burn it. Transfer the pasta to a dish, leaving behind as much of the fat as possible.

Add the onion to the pan and sauté until soft and fragrant, about 10 minutes. Add the serranos and garlic and cook 2 minutes more. Season with salt and pepper.

Stir in the tomatoes and stock, increase the heat, and as soon as the liquid reaches a rolling boil, reduce the heat to low. Simmer very gently for 15 minutes, add the pasta, and cook until it is tender, about 3 minutes. Stir in the cilantro, parsley, and lime juice; taste and correct the seasoning.

Divide the meatballs among soup bowls and ladle the hot soup over them. Sprinkle with cheese and serve immediately with tortillas and lime wedges.

To drink: Dry sherry; Mexican Beer, such as Bohemia; dry Rosé; not-too-sweet agua fresca, such as Jamaica.

Posole Rojo with Firebombs

Serves 6 to 8

Posole, a hearty Mexican soup, is a tradition among my family and friends. For years, I have been making it on Halloween. Even when I'm not planning on it, I receive requests a few days before Halloween and I always give in. Some years I made Posole Verde or Posole Blanco and sometimes I make Posole Rojo, which is the version that works best with meatballs. Typically, I cook pork butt or pork shoulder seasoned with salt and chipotle powder in a clay pot and then add it, along with its cooking juices, to the soup shortly before serving. Here, meatballs take the place of the roasted pork.

Firebombs (page 52) (see *Note*)
3 tablespoons lard or olive oil
1 large yellow onion, diced
2 serranos, stems removed, minced
6 garlic cloves
2 teaspoons dried oregano, preferably
    Mexican
Kosher salt
Black pepper in a mill
2–3 dried chiles, preferably ancho or pasilla,
    soaked in hot water, drained, peeled, and
    seeded

6 cups homemade chicken stock (page 179)
1 28-ounce can diced tomatoes, preferably
    Muir Glen brand
1 28-ounce can hominy (posole)
2 limes, cut into wedges
½ cup minced fresh cilantro leaves
½ cup minced white onion
½ cabbage, thinly shredded
3 cups (12 ounces) grated cheese, such as
    Monterey Jack
16 corn tortillas, hot
Hot sauce of choice

First, prepare the meatball mixture and, while it chills, prepare the posole.

Heat the lard or olive oil in a large soup pot set over medium heat, add the onion, and sauté until limp and fragrant, about 15 minutes; do not let the onion brown. Add the serranos and garlic, sauté 2 minutes more, and stir in the oregano. Season with salt and several turns of black pepper.

Put the dried chiles into a suribachi or molcajete and grind it into a paste. Add the chile paste, chicken stock, tomatoes, and hominy to the onion mixture. Increase the heat to high, bring to a boil, reduce the heat to low, and simmer, partially covered, for 45 minutes. Skim off any foam that forms on the surface.

While the soup cooks, finish the meatballs as described on page 52.

Gently add the meatballs to the posole and simmer for 15 minutes more.

Taste and correct the seasoning.

To serve, ladle the posole into bowls. Arrange the limes, cilantro, onion, cabbage, and cheese on a large platter and wrap the hot tortillas in a warm tea towel.

Serve the posole right away, with the condiments, tortillas, and hot sauce.

> **Note:**
> Instead of Firebombs, you can use Mexican Albondigas (page 48) or Chorizo Meatballs (page 50) in this recipe.

> **To drink:** Cold Mexican beer, such as Bohemia or Negro Modelo; Margarita; agua fresca.

Portuguese Kale Soup with Meatballs

Serves 6 to 8

This delicious soup is typically made with short ribs but it is excellent with meatballs, too. It is best in cold weather, especially in the dead of winter when you want a bone-warming soup.

Portuguese Meatballs, (page 35), uncooked
2 tablespoons olive oil, plus more as needed
2 yellow onions, diced
1 garlic bulb, cloves separated, peeled, and chopped
1 tablespoon hot Spanish paprika
3 bunches Lacinato kale, hard stems removed, leaves sliced into ½–inch crosswise strips
Red pepper flakes
Kosher salt

Black pepper in a mill
4–6 cups homemade beef stock (page 181)
2 bay leaves
3 large russet potatoes, scrubbed and cut into small dice
3 cups cooked red beans, pinto beans, or other similar beans
Sourdough hearth bread, hot
Tabasco or other hot sauce

Pour the olive oil into a large soup pot set over medium heat, add the meatballs, and brown on all sides, agitating the pan so that the balls roll. Transfer the cooked meatballs to a platter.

Put the onions in the pot, reduce the heat, and sauté until soft and fragrant, about 10 to 12 minutes; add the garlic and sauté 2 minutes more. Stir in the paprika. Add the kale and ½ cup water, increase the heat to medium, stir, cover the pan, and cook for 5 minutes. Season with salt, a few pinches of red pepper flakes, and several turns of black pepper.

Add the stock to the pot along with 4 cups of water, the bay leaves, the potatoes, and the beans. Bring to a boil, reduce the heat so that the liquid simmers gently, and skim off any foam that rises to the surface.

Simmer for 35 minutes, gently add the meatballs to the pot, and cook for 15 minutes more. Cover and let rest 10 to 15 minutes. Taste and correct for salt and pepper.

Ladle into warm soup bowls and serve with hot bread and hot sauce alongside.

To drink: Vinho Verde (Portuguese white wine, slightly effervescent).

Thai Salad with Duck Meatballs

Serves 4 to 6

Thai Lime Chile Sauce is deceptively simple, as is this salad. It has just a few ingredients, takes mere minutes to make, and is so powerfully delicious that it is almost hard to explain. It's like a magic elixir that transforms everything it touches.

Duck Meatballs (page 71), hot
Thai Lime Chile Sauce (recipe follows)
6 cups, approximately, fresh young
    salad greens

¼ cup fresh cilantro leaves
¼ cup fresh mint leaves, preferably spearmint
4 mint sprigs
1 lime, quartered

Prepare the meatballs and keep them hot.

Prepare the sauce and set it aside.

Put the salad greens, cilantro, and mint in a large bowl, add half the sauce, toss gently, and divide among individual plates.

Top each portion with some of the meatballs, garnish with a mint sprig and a lime wedge, and serve immediately.

Thai Lime Chile Sauce
Makes about ¼ cup

5 garlic cloves, minced
3–4 serranos, minced
1 tablespoon fish sauce

2 tablespoons fresh lime juice
    (from 1–2 limes)
2 teaspoons sugar

Combine all ingredients in a small bowl and stir until the sugar is dissolved. Set aside until ready to use.

Variation: Instead of the duck meatballs, use the Spicy Thai Meatballs (page 56).

To drink: Young coconut juice; unsweetened iced tea; Gewürztraminer.

Roasted Tomato & Eggplant Soup with Lamb Meatballs

Serves 6 to 8

Because my younger daughter, Nicolle, loves both eggplant and lamb, I'm always searching for new ways to prepare them for her. This soup came about almost accidentally, when I happened to have all the ingredients in my refrigerator at one time but no specific plans for them. It is now a favorite.

Lemon Lamb Meatballs (page 42)
2 medium-large eggplant
5 large tomatoes
Olive oil
Kosher salt
1 large yellow onion, minced
4 garlic cloves, minced
1 bay leaf
1 quart chicken or beef stock (pages 179, 181)
Black pepper in a mill
Grated zest of 1 lemon
1 tablespoon fresh snipped chives or Italian
   parsley

Make the meatballs and set them aside; this can be done a day in advance. If made in advance, remove them from the refrigerator when you start to prepare the soup.

Preheat the oven to 350 degrees.

Cut the eggplant in half lengthwise and cut the tomatoes in half crosswise, through their equators. Set them on a baking sheet and brush the cut surfaces generously with olive oil. Season all over with salt.

Roast in the oven until the eggplant is tender when pierced with a fork and the tomatoes are lightly browned. Remove from the oven and let cool.

While the vegetables cool, pour a little olive oil into a heavy soup pot, add the onion, and set over medium-low heat. Cook very gently until the onion is soft and fragrant, about 25 minutes. Do not let it brown. Add the garlic and sauté 2 minutes more.

Peel the cooled eggplant, chop it, and add it to the cooked onions.

Press the tomatoes through a fine sieve or food mill fitted with the small blade, discard the skins and seeds, and stir the meat and juices into the eggplant mixture.

Season with salt.

Pour the stock into the soup, add the bay leaf, bring to a boil, reduce the heat, and simmer gently for 30 minutes. Remove from the heat and let cool slightly.

Use tongs to retrieve and discard the bay leaf.

Use an immersion blender to purée the soup until it is smooth and creamy; if it seems a bit too thick, thin with a little water to reach the desired consistency.

Return the soup to low heat, season generously with several turns of black pepper, taste, and correct for salt, if needed.

Carefully lower the meatballs into the soup and simmer gently for 10 minutes.

To serve, ladle into soup plates, dividing the meatballs evenly between portions.

Sprinkle a little lemon zest and chives or parsley over the soup and serve immediately.

Potato Salad with Fresh Herb Meatballs

Serves 6 to 8

If you usually enjoy meatballs in their typical contexts—in red sauce, with spaghetti or other pasta and on sandwiches, you are in for a treat when you add them to a salad. Here, they make a full meal out of a tangy potato salad. I love the way the fresh herbs resonate with the other flavors in this dish but any well-made meatball will be delicious.

Fresh Herb Meatballs (page 45)
2 pounds red potatoes, scrubbed clean but not peeled
Kosher salt
1 shallot, minced
4 or 5 radishes, trimmed and minced
2 garlic cloves, minced
4 tablespoons champagne or white wine vinegar
1 tablespoon freshly squeezed lemon juice
3 tablespoons fresh snipped chives

Black pepper in a mill
⅔ cup extra-virgin olive oil, plus more as needed
1 bunch French breakfast radishes, leaves separated, thinly sliced
1 bunch radish leaves, cut into very thin ribbons
1 small red onion, peeled and thinly sliced
8 ounces very small Blue Lake green beans, blanched
3 tablespoons Italian parsley

First, make the meatball mixture and while it chills, prepare the salad.

Put the potatoes into a large saucepan, cover with water by at least 2 inches and season generously with salt. Bring to a boil and cook until the potatoes are tender but not mushy. Drain and transfer to a wide shallow bowl to cool slightly.

Meanwhile, make the vinaigrette. Put the shallot, minced radishes and garlic into a bowl, season with salt, add the vinegar and lemon juice and set aside for a few minutes. Add the chives, season with several turns of black pepper and stir in the olive oil. Taste and correct for acid and salt. Set aside.

When the potatoes are cool enough to handle, slice them thinly and put them in a wide shallow serving bowl. Spoon about half the dressing over the potatoes and set aside.

Cook the meatballs according to the directions in that recipe. While the meatballs rest, briefly, add the radishes, radish leaves, and green beans to the potatoes and toss gently.

Scatter the meatballs on top of the salad and spoon the remaining dressing over everything. Season with salt and pepper, sprinkle with Italian parsley and serve immediately.

Alternately, the salad can be served on individual plates.

To drink: Iced tea (unsweetened); beer.

Bread Salad with Meatballs

Serves 6 to 8

This salad is inspired by fattoush, a Middle Eastern bread salad that uses pita bread and sumac, a tangy spice suggestive of lemon; za'atar is simply sumac with salt and toasted and ground sesame seeds, which contributes an earthy flavor.

Lemon Lamb Meatballs (page 42) or
   Moroccan Merguez Meatballs (page 62)
4–6 stale pita breads or slices of hearth bread,
   in bite-sized pieces, lightly toasted
   (see *Note* on next page)
1 small shallot, minced
3 garlic cloves, minced
2 tablespoons freshly squeezed lemon juice
1 tablespoon best-quality white wine vinegar
1 teaspoon dried oregano
1 teaspoon ground sumac or za'atar, optional
Kosher salt
Black pepper in a mill

6 to 8 tablespoons extra-virgin olive oil
3 medium heirloom tomatoes, cored,
   halved (through the equator) and
   cut into wedges
½ small red onion, peeled and cut into thin
   lengthwise slices
1 small cucumber, peeled, seeded and cut
   into thin half moons
½ cup green olives, pitted and sliced
   lengthwise
2 teaspoons capers
6 ounces feta cheese, broken into chunks
3 generous handfuls of small-leafed arugula

Make the meatball mixture and while it chills, prepare the salad.

Put the bread into a wide shallow bowl and set it aside.

Put the shallot and garlic into a small bowl, add the lemon juice, vinegar, oregano and sumac or za'atar, if using, and season with salt and pepper. Set aside for about 15 minutes while you prepare the vegetables.

Pour the olive oil into the shallot mixture, taste and correct for salt, pepper and acid balance.

Reserve about 3 tablespoons of the dressing and pour the rest over the bread and toss.

Add the tomatoes, onion, cucumber, olives, capers and cheese and toss again. Let rest for 15 minutes, while you cook the meatballs.

Put the arugula in a bowl, season with salt and toss. Divide among individual bowls or plates. Top with the salad, add several meatballs, drizzle the reserved dressing on top and serve.

> *Note:*
> If you do not have stale bread, tear or cut fresh bread (either pita or hearth) into bite-sized pieces and toast it in a slow oven, turning it now and then until it is lightly browned and crunchy.

> *To drink:* Hard cider; ice-cold pilsner; dry sparkling wine, such as Spanish cava.

Meatball Tacos

Serves 2 to 4

Although it is not traditional, I like to put the cheese directly on top of hot tortillas so as it melts, it forms a sort of blanket around the meatballs; it also helps hold everything in place.

4 medium corn tortillas, preferably handmade
2 cups thinly shredded cabbage
¼ cup chopped cilantro leaves
1 serrano, seeded and minced
Kosher salt
1 lime, halved
8–10 ounces grated cheese, such as
    Monterey Jack

12–16 Mexican Albondigas (page 48),
    Chorizo Meatballs (page 50), or
    Firebombs (page 52) hot
2 or 3 small radishes, shaved thin with a
    vegetable peeler
Hot sauce of choice

Heat a large, heavy skillet or a stove top griddle and, when it is hot, heat the tortillas until very soft and pliable; do not let them burn or turn crisp.

Working quickly, put the cabbage, cilantro, and serrano in a bowl, season with salt, and squeeze in the juice of half the lime.

When the tortillas are hot, top each one with cheese and, the moment it melts, transfer to individual plates (1 or 2 per serving). Divide the hot meatballs among the servings and squeeze a little lime juice over them. Top with the cabbage mixture and the radishes, season with a little more salt, and serve immediately with hot sauce.

> **To drink:** Agua fresca; ice-cold Bohemia or other Mexican beer.

A Classic Meatball Sandwich, with Variations

Makes 1, easily increased

The best time to make a meatball sandwich is, of course, when you have leftover meatballs, which is one of the reasons I prefer smaller meatballs—they are easier to use on sandwiches. I like to borrow a trick from banh mi, those fabulous Vietnamese sandwiches. Traditional banh mi are made on bread very much like our soft french rolls, with some of the soft inner bread pulled out to form a sort of boat to hold the ingredients. This is a perfect technique for meatball sandwiches, as you can actually get your mouth around them without the meatballs popping out the side or the other end.

If you have a toaster oven, this is the time to use it, as it is a waste of energy to heat an entire oven for one sandwich.

1 soft french roll
Olive oil
Sautéed onions, onion jam, or onion
    marmalade
3–5 leftover meatballs, either The Meatball
    (page 24), Roasted Garlic Meatballs
(page 27), or Bolognese-style Meatballs
(page 31), reheated
2–3 ounces grated Monterey Jack, Mozzarella
    Fresca, or other good melting cheese
Chopped Italian parsley

Preheat a toaster oven or regular oven broiler.

Slice or pull open the french roll and use your fingers to pull out about half of the soft parts of bread on both pieces.

Brush both sides of the bread with olive oil and toast or broil until lightly browned.

Set the toasted bread on a clean work surface and spread the onions, onion jam, or onion marmalade over the bottom piece. Top with the meatballs and scatter the cheese on top. Set, open-faced, in the toaster oven or oven broiler until the cheese melts.

Sprinkle Italian parsley on top of the cheese, close the sandwich, and enjoy.

Variations:

Roasted Sweet Pepper & Meatball Sandwich: Add about ½ cup roasted, peeled, and julienned sweet peppers on top of the onions and continue as directed in the main recipe.

Meatballs Marinara Sandwich: Use the meatballs and sauce from Tom's Garlic Turkey Meatballs (page 161), Summertime Spaghetti & Meatballs (page 167), Halloween Spaghetti & Meatballs (page 168), or Gudene (page 163) to make the sandwich.

Thanksgiving Meatball Sandwich: Spread old-fashioned (gum-free) cream cheese over the bottom half of the toasted bread, top it with cranberry relish or cranberry salsa, and top with turkey meatballs (page 161).

Hawaiian Meatball Sandwich: Spread mayonnaise over the bottom half of the bread, top with sautéed cabbage and 3 or 4 Hawaiian meatballs and season with chile water (page 151).

To drink: Lemonade, iced tea, milk, beer.

Polish Meatballs with Wild Mushroom Sauce

Serves 3 to 4

In Poland, meatballs are known as klopsiki *and are frequently served in a sour cream sauce thickened with flour; meatballs with mushroom gravy, also thickened with flour, are common, too. This version, while not 100 percent traditional, is based on the classic preparation but without the flour.*

1¼ cups stale bread, torn in pieces
½ cup heavy cream
2 tablespoons butter
1 small white or yellow onion, grated
Kosher salt
¾ pound pastured pork butt or shoulder, ground
¾ pound grass-fed beef, ground
Black pepper in a mill
½ teaspoon caraway seed

3 tablespoons chopped Italian parsley
1 egg yolk, beaten
1 egg white, whipped until it forms soft peaks
6 ounces maitake or oyster mushrooms, torn into bite-sized pieces
¾ cup dry white wine
1 tablespoon freshly squeezed lemon juice
4 ounces crème fraîche or sour cream

Put the bread into a mixing bowl, add the cream, and set aside.

Put half the butter into a small sauté pan set over medium heat and, when the butter is melted, add the onion and simmer gently until fragrant, about 5 minutes; do not let it brown. Season with salt and set aside to cool.

Use a fork to break up the bread a bit. Add the pork and beef, season with salt, several turns of black pepper, the caraway seed, and 2 tablespoons of the parsley and mix thoroughly. Add the egg yolk and mix again. Use a large rubber spatula to fold in the egg white, being careful not to overmix.

Cover and refrigerate for an hour.

To finish the meatballs, preheat the oven to 325 degrees.

Use a 1½-ounce ice cream scoop to form balls and set each ball into a large ovenproof skillet. When all the balls have been formed, set the skillet on the middle rack of the oven and bake for 15 minutes. Open the oven, rotate the meatballs, and cook 15 minutes longer.

Remove from the oven, transfer the meatballs to a platter, cover, and keep warm.

Set the skillet over medium heat, add the remaining butter to the pan drippings, and add the mushrooms when it is melted. Use a spatula to turn the mushrooms in the butter, season with salt, add the wine, cover, and simmer until the mushrooms are wilted, about 5 minutes. Uncover, increase the heat to high, and simmer until the liquid is nearly completely reduced. Add the lemon juice, stir in the crème fraîche or sour cream, and heat through. Season very generously with black pepper and stir in the remaining parsley.

Carefully tip the meatballs back into the skillet, along with any juices that have collected on the platter. Turn them gently in the sauce.

Serve immediately or cool, refrigerate, and reheat the next day.

> **Serving Suggestions:** Spoon over egg noodles, mashed potatoes, potato pancakes, or barley grits.
>
> **To drink:** When served as an appetizer, enjoy with chilled vodka.

Moroccan Meatball Tagine with Parsley Couscous & Harissa

Serves 4 to 6

There is no real shortcut when it comes to a tagine, though the preparation involved is not difficult. There are simply many elements, including harissa, a classic and essential condiment in Moroccan cuisine. The version here is not too fiery, as I wanted this dish to be wine-friendly, which it is. You can easily make both the harissa and the meatballs a day or two before serving the tagine, but you must prepare the couscous shortly before serving it. If you like preserved lemons and have some on hand, slice a few wedges thinly and serve them with the harissa. I also like to have a bowl of thick, whole milk yogurt as a condiment, too.

Harissa (recipe follows)
Moroccan Merguez Meatballs (page 62)
3 tablespoons ghee or smen (page 174)
1 small yellow onion, grated
5 or 6 garlic cloves, minced
Kosher salt
Black pepper in a mill
2 teaspoons grated fresh ginger
1 teaspoon ground turmeric
1 teaspoon ground cumin
1 teaspoon hot paprika
1 teaspoon sweet paprika
½ teaspoon crushed red pepper flakes
1½ cups chicken stock (page 179)
A few saffron threads
2 tablespoons hot water
½ cup chopped fresh cilantro
¼ cup chopped fresh Italian parsley
Parsley Couscous (recipe follows)
⅓ cup freshly squeezed lemon juice

First, make the harissa; this can be done a day or two in advance.

Make the meatballs but leave them neat, without caul fat or rice flour; do not cook them. Simply shape them, set them on wax paper, and refrigerate.

Put the ghee or smen into a large, deep sauté pan set over medium heat, add the onion, and sauté until fragrant, about 7 or 8 minutes. Add the garlic and sauté 2 minutes more. Season with salt and several turns of black pepper.

Add the ginger, turmeric, cumin, paprikas, and crushed red pepper flakes, stir, and cook for 2 minutes. Add the chicken stock, bring to a boil, lower the heat so that the liquid simmers gently, cover the pan, and cook for 15 minutes.

Meanwhile, put the saffron into a small bowl and cover with the hot water.

Prepare the couscous for steaming.

After 15 minutes, stir the saffron and the water into the sauce. Carefully add the meatballs and 1 cup of water so that the liquid covers them. Without stirring, cover the pan and simmer gently for 30 minutes.

Finish steaming the couscous and tip it into a large, shallow serving bowl.

Working quickly, use a slotted spoon to move the meatballs from the sauce to the top of the couscous.

Stir the cilantro and parsley into the sauce, increase the heat, and reduce it by about one quarter. Remove from the heat, add the lemon juice, taste, and correct for salt. Pour the sauce over the meatballs and couscous and serve immediately with the harissa.

Harissa
Makes about ¼ cup

1½ ounces dried chiles, preferably anchos	2 teaspoons kosher salt, plus more as need
1 tablespoon cumin seed, lightly toasted	½ cup extra-virgin olive oil
2 teaspoons coriander seed	½ cup fresh lemon juice
1 teaspoon caraway seed	2 tablespoons minced cilantro leaves
6 garlic cloves, crushed	2 tablespoons Italian parsley leaves

Heat a heavy pan—cast iron is ideal—over a high flame, add the chiles and toast, turning frequently, until they puff up with fragrant steam; transfer to a work surface to cool. Remove the stems and seed cores.

Grind the cumin, coriander, and caraway seeds in an electric spice grinder or suribachi.

Put the chiles, ground seeds, garlic, and salt into the work bowl of a food processor and pulse until the ingredients form a very thick, smooth paste. Transfer to a medium bowl, stir in the olive oil and lemon juice, taste, and correct for salt. Add the cilantro and parsley immediately before serving.

The paste can be stored in the refrigerator for several weeks; once the olive oil and lemon juice have been added, use within 3 or 4 days.

Parsley Couscous
Makes about 3 cups

The designation "instant couscous" is misleading; virtually all couscous in the United States is the dried version that is sometimes identified in this way. It is always better (and easier to digest) when steamed in this fashion.

1 cup couscous	2 tablespoons minced fresh cilantro leaves
3 tablespoons smen	2 tablespoons minced fresh Italian parsley

Put the couscous in a medium bowl and pour ¾ cup of water over it. Let sit until all the water is absorbed, about 10 minutes. Put the couscous in a colander or strainer with small enough holes to contain it; set the colander or strainer in a pot filled with about 3 inches of water. Tuck a damp towel into the space between the colander and the pot and set over high heat, uncovered, for 10 minutes, until steam rises the couscous.

Remove the couscous from the heat, set the colander on a work surface, and drizzle a cup of water over the couscous, raking it with a fork all the while. Return the colander to the pot and steam again, until the couscous is about 3 times its original size.

Put the couscous in a wide, shallow serving bowl, add the smen, cilantro, and parsley and fluff with a fork. Cover with a towel or aluminum foil until ready to serve.

To drink: Iced tea; a Moroccan white wine or other light, refreshing white, such as Albariño, Arneis Vermentino or Gruner-Veltliner.

Three-Peppercorn Meatballs in Peppercorn Sauce

Makes 24 meatballs

These yummy little morsels began as meatloaf inspired by the beautifully fragrant peppercorns—black, white, and green—from Sarawak, one of two Malaysian states on the island of Borneo. These days, I prefer the meatballs as I like the way flavors blossom when more of the meat comes in direct contact with the heat.

2 tablespoons olive oil
2 shallots, minced
5 or 6 garlic cloves, minced
Kosher salt
2 teaspoons black peppercorns, crushed
2 teaspoons white peppercorns, crushed
2 teaspoons dried green peppercorns, crushed
½ teaspoon ground cardamom

¾ pound grass-fed beef, ground twice
¾ pound pastured pork, ground twice
⅓ cup chopped fresh Italian parsley
1 large egg, beaten
4–6 ounces caul fat
½ cup Armagnac or brandy
1 tablespoon brined green peppercorns
6 tablespoons crème fraîche

Pour the olive oil into a sauté pan set over medium heat, add the shallots, and sauté until soft and fragrant, about 7 minutes. Add the garlic and sauté 1 minute more.

Season with salt.

Stir in the black, white, and green peppercorns and the cardamom, remove from the heat, and let cool.

Put the beef and pork into a mixing bowl and add the cooled shallot mixture and the parsley. Mix thoroughly. Add the egg, mix well, and then use your hands to knead the mixture until it is uniformly smooth. Cover and refrigerate.

To finish the meatballs, line a baking sheet with wax paper.

Use a ¾-ounce ice cream scoop or melon baller to form balls, returning them to the wax paper after they are formed.

Stretch the caul fat on a clean work surface and wrap each ball in a piece of it.

Set a heavy skillet—cast iron is ideal—over medium-high heat and, when the pan is hot, add several meatballs. Cook for about 45 seconds, agitate the skillet so the balls roll, and cook until evenly browned and starting to firm up. Transfer to a plate and continue until all the balls have been cooked.

Pour the Armagnac or brandy into the pan and swirl to deglaze it, using a fork or spatula to pick up any bits of meat that stick. Add the brined green peppercorns and the crème fraîche, stir and heat through, and carefully return the meatballs and any juices that have collected on the plate to the pan. Lower the heat, cover, and simmer gently for 5 minutes.

Remove from the heat, tip into a shallow serving bowl, and serve immediately.

> **Variation:**
> **Green Peppercorn Mustard Meatballs:** Add 1 tablespoon green peppercorn mustard to the meat mixture along with the egg. Add another tablespoon of the mustard to the sauce along with the crème fraîche.

> **Serving Suggestions:** With sliced baguette, lightly toasted, as an appetizer; as a main course with mashed potatoes, fresh fettuccine, or pappardelle.
>
> **To drink:** Malaysian-style (salted) limeade; savory spiced lassi.

Hawaiian Meatballs with Cabbage, Chile Water & Grilled Pineapple

Serves 6 to 8

Most Hawaiian meatballs are served in a teriyaki or similar sauce and, to my palate, are among the least interesting selections in a luau. Kalua pig is generally the centerpiece of a Hawaiian feast and when there is any left over, you can use it to make meatballs. But you don't have to wait until your next luau to do so. You can make meatballs using the same flavorings as kalua pig, salt, and, unless you're cooking in an underground imu, liquid smoke. What could be easier?

Please note that to serve these meatballs with the chile water, you'll need to prepare the water at least two days in advance, but don't worry—it takes mere minutes to do; most of the time is to allow the flavors to blossom. You rarely see hot chiles or hot sauce on Hawaiian tables, but chile water is common and it adds a bright flash of refreshing heat.

Hawaiian Chile Water (recipe follows)
2 tablespoons lard or olive oil
6 cups finely shredded cabbage
1 small white or yellow onion, grated
2 pounds pastured pork shoulder or butt, ground
1 tablespoon natural liquid smoke

1 tablespoon salt, preferably Hawaiian alaea, crushed, plus more as needed
Black pepper in a mill
6–8 ounces caul fat
1 pineapple, peeled, cored, and cut into ¾-inch thick rounds
Steamed white rice, hot

Put the lard or olive oil into a heavy skillet set over medium heat. Set aside 4 cups of cabbage and sauté the remaining 2 cups in the hot fat until it is limp. Add the grated onion and sauté 5 or 6 minutes more. Remove from the heat and let cool.

Put the ground pork into a large mixing bowl, add the cooled cabbage, the liquid smoke, the 1 tablespoon of salt, and several turns of black pepper. Mix thoroughly and refrigerate for at least 1 hour or as long as overnight.

To finish the meatballs, cover a baking sheet with wax paper and prepare a fire in an outdoor grill or preheat a stove top grill.

Use a 1½-ounce ice cream scoop to form meatballs and set each one on the wax paper.

Spread caul fat over a clean work surface, wrap each ball, and return it to the wax paper.

Set a heavy skillet over medium heat and, when the pan is hot, add several meatballs, cook for 45 seconds, agitate the pan, and continue to cook until they are evenly browned and beginning to firm up. Transfer the cooked balls to absorbent paper and continue until all the meatballs have been cooked.

Working quickly, add the reserved cabbage to the skillet, where there should be plenty of fragrant pan drippings. Sauté and toss for about 2 minutes. Return the meatballs to the pan, setting them on top the cabbage. Cover, lower the heat, and simmer gently while you prepare the pineapple.

Put the pineapple on the grill and season it with a little salt; cook for 2 minutes, turn, and cook for 2 to 3 minutes more. Transfer to a serving platter and season all over with freshly ground pepper.

Transfer the meatballs and cabbage to a serving platter.

Serve immediately with the steamed rice, Hawaiian potato salad, or potato-mac salad and the chile water on the side.

Hawaiian Chile Water
Makes 2 cups

2 teaspoons Hawaiian alaea or kosher salt
2 teaspoons white wine vinegar
1 garlic clove, crushed

6–8 hot chile peppers (cayenne, Thai, serrano, or others)

Wash a tall 16-ounce glass bottle thoroughly in hot water and let it dry.

Put the salt, vinegar, garlic, and chiles into the bottle and fill with tap water, filtered water, or spring water. Close tightly, shake, and refrigerate for at least 2 days.

The chile water will keep for several weeks in the refrigerator. It is excellent on rice, kalua pig, baked sweet potatoes, and many other foods, including these meatballs.

To drink: Young coconut juice; ice-cold root beer; ice-cold pilsner.

Curried Chicken Meatballs with Chutney & Yogurt Turmeric Sauce

Makes about 24 meatballs

I have a special fondness for and understanding of Indian flavors, as India was the first country I visited (other than a short jaunt to Victoria on Vancouver Island). For several weeks, I stayed in a village about 200 kilometers inland from what is now known as Mumbai but was then Bombay. I spent part of my stay in a private home with a cook who lived on the grounds. Although we did not speak each other's language, she understood quickly that I was as interested in being with her in the kitchen as I was in being fed at the dining room table. She humored me and taught me several simple techniques, including preparing spice mixtures from whole spices and frying them in ghee before adding other ingredients so that they lose their raw taste and their flavors blossom. All these years later, Indian cuisines—and there are many—remain among my favorites.

4 tablespoons clarified butter (ghee)
(page 174)
1 shallot, minced
2 garlic cloves, minced
Kosher salt
Black pepper in a mill
1 tablespoon freshly grated ginger
3 teaspoons ground turmeric
2 teaspoons coriander seed, ground
1 teaspoon cumin seed, toasted and ground
1½ teaspoons ground cardamom

1½ teaspoons ground cayenne
½ teaspoon cinnamon
½ teaspoon freshly grated nutmeg
1 pound chicken thigh meat, ground twice
1 egg, beaten
⅓ cup chopped fresh cilantro
3–4 ounces caul fat
¾ cup whole milk yogurt
½ cup white wine, chicken stock, or water
Chutney of choice

Pour 3 tablespoons of the clarified butter into a small sauté pan set over medium heat, add the shallot, and cook until soft, about 6 minutes; add the garlic and sauté 1 minute more.

Season with salt and pepper.

Add the ginger, 2 tablespoons of the turmeric, the coriander, 1 teaspoon of the cardamom, 1 teaspoon of the cayenne, the cinnamon, and the nutmeg and cook gently, stirring constantly, for 2 minutes.

Remove from the heat and let cool.

Put the chicken into a medium bowl, add the cooled spice mixture and the egg, and mix thoroughly. Mix in half the cilantro.

Cover and refrigerate for 30 minutes.

While the meatball mixture chills, prepare the sauce. Put the yogurt into a small bowl, add the remaining turmeric, cayenne, cardamom, and cilantro, season with salt and pepper, and stir well. Taste and correct for salt. Cover and refrigerate.

To finish the meatballs, set wax paper on a sheet pan and spread the caul fat on a clean work surface.

Use a ¾-ounce ice cream scoop or melon baller to form balls and set each one on the wax paper.

Wrap each ball in caul fat, return to the wax paper and, when all balls have been wrapped, cover lightly and refrigerate for 30 minutes.

Pour the remaining clarified butter into a large, heavy skillet and cook the balls, a few at a time, until they are evenly browned and somewhat firm.

When all have been browned, return them to the pan, add the wine, chicken stock or water, and agitate the pan until the liquid is nearly completely reduced. Lower the heat, cover the pan, and cook for about 7 minutes, until the balls are cooked through.

Remove from the heat and let rest for 5 minutes.

Transfer to a platter and serve immediately with toothpicks, chutney, and the yogurt sauce.

> **Variation:**
> **In Coconut Sauce:** When all of the meatballs have been cooked and returned to the pan, add 1 cup chicken stock and 1 cup coconut milk, bring to a boil, reduce the heat, cover, and simmer for 10 minutes. Uncover and reduce the sauce by about one-third. Serve over steamed rice with chutney.

Serving Suggestions: Over rice or quinoa; over or alongside vegetable biryani; wrapped in flatbread and topped with a drizzle of yogurt sauce and a dollop of chutney.

To drink: Gewürztraminer; Riesling; Vinho Verde.

Curried Chicken Meatballs with Chutney & Yogurt Turmeric Sauce   **155**

Lamb Meatballs Dijonnaise

Makes about 20 to 24 small meatballs

Chicken Dijonnaise is a classic French dish from Dijon, home of one of the world's greatest mustards. As delicious as mustard is with chicken, I think it is even better with lamb and so I took inspiration from the flavors of the traditional dish and applied them to lamb meatballs, best served as an appetizer, with the Dijon sauce on the side for dipping. For a main course version, see the Variation at the end of this recipe.

2 tablespoons olive oil, plus more for frying
2 shallots, minced
3 garlic cloves, preferably fresh, minced
Kosher salt
Black pepper in a mill
5 tablespoons Dijon mustard
1½ pounds lamb shoulder or leg, ground

1½ cups (6 ounces) Gruyere, grated
1 large egg, preferably pastured, beaten
2 teaspoons fresh thyme leaves
1 tablespoon chopped fresh Italian parsley
½ cup all-purpose flour
2 tablespoons crème fraîche or sour cream

Put the olive oil into a small sauté pan set over medium-low heat, add the shallots, and sauté until soft and fragrant, about 7 minutes. Add the garlic and sauté 2 minutes more. Season with salt and pepper, stir in 1 tablespoon of the mustard, and remove from the heat. Let cool for a few minutes.

Break up the lamb and put it into a medium mixing bowl. Add the shallot mixture, half the cheese, the egg, half the thyme leaves, and the parsley. Season with salt and several generous turns of black pepper and mix thoroughly.

Preheat the oven to 325 degrees.

Put the flour in a medium bowl.

Cover a baking sheet with wax paper.

Use a 1-ounce ice cream scoop to shape the meatballs, setting each one on the wax paper.

Put 2 or 3 meatballs into the bowl with the flour, agitate the bowl to coat the meatballs evenly with flour. Set the floured meatballs on the wax paper.

Pour a bit of oil into a heavy sauté pan or nonstick pan set over medium heat. Fry the meatballs, agitating the pan so that they brown evenly all over. Transfer the cooked meatballs to a baking dish just big enough to hold them in a single layer.

When all of the meatballs have been fried, scatter the remaining cheese over them and bake for about 12 minutes, until the cheese is fully melted and bubbly and the meatballs are cooked through.

Meanwhile, put the remaining mustard in a small bowl, add the remaining thyme leaves and the crème fraîche or sour cream, stir, taste, and correct for salt and pepper as needed.

Serve the meatballs hot from the oven, in the baking dish, with the Dijon sauce and plenty of toothpicks.

> **Variation:**
>
> For a delicious main course, return the sauté pan to medium heat after transferring the meatballs to a baking dish. Add ¾ cup chicken or duck stock to the pan, swirl the pan to pick up bits of meat and simmer until the liquid reduces by about a third. Add the remaining mustard and the crème fraîche, heat through and stir in the remaining cheese and thyme. Season with several turns of black pepper, pour over the meatballs and set under a hot broiler until the sauce bubbles and the meatballs are cooked through, about 10 minutes.

> ***Serving Suggestions:*** As an appetizer; as a main course, with roasted potatoes or steamed rice; on sandwiches using warm sourdough baguettes.
>
> ***To drink:*** French or French-style pinot noir; Russian River Valley pinot noir; sparkling wine.

Marlena's Veal & Ricotta Meatballs with Tomatoes & Piselli

Serves 4

Marlena Spieler is a friend and colleague who has written many wonderful cookbooks. I've enjoyed her polpettini—delicious little meatballs she cooked up for Marcy Smothers, author of Snacks: Adventures in Food, Aisle by Aisle *(Harper Collins, 2013)—one night in Marcy's kitchen. When I set out to write this book, I asked Marlena to contribute a recipe and this is it. These ethereal spheres are from her meatball cookbook, as yet unwritten. If you do not want to use veal, Marlena says, pork works just fine.*

1 slice stale bread, such as pain levain, in pieces
½ cup milk
1 pound ground veal
8 ounces whole milk ricotta
1 small red onion, minced
3 garlic cloves, minced
2 teaspoons minced fresh Italian parsley
1 teaspoon fresh thyme leaves
½ teaspoon herbes de Provence
Pinch of nutmeg

Pinch of ground allspice
Kosher salt
Black pepper in a mill
2 tablespoons olive oil
1 cup chicken or beef stock (pages 179, 181)
1 cup shelled English peas
1½ cups chopped tomatoes or 1 14-ounce can diced tomatoes
¼ cup (1 ounce) freshly grated Parmigiano-Reggiano

Put the bread in a small bowl, add the milk, and let soak until softened.

Meanwhile, put the veal, ricotta, onion, garlic, parsley, thyme, herbs de Provence, nutmeg, and allspice in a medium bowl.

Use a fork to break up the bread, squeeze out the milk, and add the bread to the bowl.

Mix thoroughly, season with salt and several generous turns of black pepper, and mix again.

Refrigerate for 1 hour.

Cover a baking sheet with wax paper.

To finish, use a 1-ounce ice cream scoop to form balls; set the balls on the wax paper.

Set a medium sauté pan over medium heat and, when the pan is hot, add several meatballs and cook for 45 seconds. Gently agitate the pan so that the meatballs roll and continue cooking them until they are evenly browned all over and have begun to set up. Return the cooked meatballs to the wax paper and continue until all meatballs are cooked.

Pour the stock into the pan, swirl to deglaze it, and use a spatula to scrape up any bits of meat that stick. Add the peas and tomatoes and simmer gently for 3 to 4 minutes. Gently return the meatballs to the pan, cover, and simmer for 5 minutes, until the meatballs are cooked through.

Divide among individual soup plates, sprinkle some Parmigiano-Reggiano over each portion, and serve immediately.

To drink: Prosecco.

Tom's Garlic Turkey Meatballs in Tomato Sauce

Serves 6

Thomas O'Brien, my son-in-law, is a great cook. He cooks, as most home cooks do most of the time, without following recipes. In this dish, Tom says you can use other meat—pork, beef, even lamb—but that there is something about the way the fat of the turkey infuses the sauce that results in a rich lusciousness. Don't use good wine in the sauce; he insists and even suggests using a wine that is corked. I haven't tried that yet, but I have tried these meatballs and they are every bit as good as he promises. Finally, don't be shocked by the full cup of minced garlic. That is indeed how much Tom uses, though he says you can probably get by with one-half cup if you prefer.

1 slice of bacon, chopped
1 tablespoon olive oil
3 garlic cloves
2 28-ounce cans crushed tomatoes, preferably Muir Glen brand, + 1 14-ounce can, if needed
5 teaspoons dried herb mixture (see *Note* on next page)
1½ pounds ground turkey thigh (15–25 percent fat)
1½ cups (6 ounces) grated Romano cheese

1 cup minced garlic cloves
½ cup fresh bread crumbs
1 tablespoon red pepper flakes
2 small eggs, beaten
Kosher salt
Black pepper in a mill
1 tablespoon + ½ teaspoon Worcestershire sauce
1 teaspoon Tabasco or Crystal hot sauce
1 cup red wine

Put the bacon and olive oil into a large, deep skillet—a Dutch oven is ideal—add the garlic, and sauté gently over medium heat until the garlic takes on just a bit of color, about 1½ minutes. Add the tomatoes and 1 teaspoon of the herb mixture. Bring to a boil, reduce the heat, and simmer very gently.

To make the meatballs, put the turkey in a large mixing bowl and add the cheese, minced garlic, bread crumbs, eggs, red pepper flakes, and the remaining herb mixture. Add the tablespoon of Worcestershire sauce, season with salt and pepper, and mix thoroughly.

Refrigerate for 30 minutes.

Shape the mixture in balls about the size and shape of large chicken eggs; wetting your palms between each one will keep them from sticking. When all the balls have been shaped, drop them gently into the sauce, making sure to leave space between each one. Do not stir or otherwise touch the balls for 20 to 30 minutes, until they have firmed up.

If the sauce does not cover the meatballs, gently tip in the 14-ounce can. Agitate the pan slightly to distribute it.

Once the meatballs firm up, stir the sauce gently and turn each meatball over, being certain not to break it.

Add the hot sauce and the red wine and again agitate the pan gently. Simmer for 30 minutes and remove from heat.

Cool completely, cover, and refrigerate overnight. Reheat over low heat until the meatballs are completely hot, taste the sauce, and correct for salt and pepper.

Serve neat or over pasta, polenta, or barley.

> **Note:**
> To make the herb mixture, combine 1¼ teaspoons each of dried marjoram, dried basil, dried thyme, and dried parsley. If you prefer to use fresh herbs, use 2 teaspoons of each of them.

> **To drink:** Rustic or even homemade red wine.

Gudene: Spaghetti
with Stuffed Pig Skin Rolls, Meatballs & Italian Sausage

Serves 10 to 12

This dish is, at a minimum, a two-day project, one day for shopping, a second day for preparation. If you prefer, you can spread the preparation over two days, as well, and serve on the third. It is a fun activity for a group, which I organized one New Year's Eve. While the gudene cooked, we watched The Godfather I *and God-father II,* which several of the guests had, remarkably, not seen, and we ate well after we rang in the New Year.

My most memorable Gudene dinner was in the mid-1990s, not long after a friend shared his mother's recipe. My friend Mike Thompson, then a state senator and now a member of Congress, invited Francis and Eleanor Coppola to dinner at his St. Helena home so that I could serve this dish. When Francis arrived, he walked over to the stove where I was stirring the sauce, took the spoon from my hand, reached down into the rich sauce, pulled out a pork roll, exclaimed, "Codene!" and asked me about my recipe. His mother made it, he said, the Neopolitan way, filling the pork skins with garlic, raisins, and chopped hard-boiled eggs. My version came from Sicily. I brought a menu with me, which Francis signed just before we all went home. "Ya did good, kid!" he wrote. I framed it and it hangs on my office wall.

In the version from my friend, the meatballs were flat, more like rectangular beef patties than what we think of as meatballs. With all due apologies to Venera, my friend's mother, I have added a personal touch by making round meatballs, in part because the flat "meatballs" can fall apart in the sauce and in part because the round ones are a bit smaller. This is a big, rich meal.

for the pork skin rolls
2 sheets of pork skin, trimmed and cut into
    rectangles about 8 inches by 10 inches
Kosher salt
Black pepper in a mill
1 garlic bulb, cloves separated, crushed,
    and minced
Zest of 2 lemons, finely grated
1 small bunch Italian parsley, minced
½ cup shelled pine nuts

Kitchen twine
Olive oil

for the sauce
1 onion, diced
8 whole garlic cloves
Kosher salt
Black pepper in a mill
3 large (28-ounce) cans crushed or diced
    tomatoes, preferably Muir Glen brand

2 small cans (6 ounces) tomato paste
2 teaspoons dried basil
2 teaspoons dried oregano
1 teaspoon crushed red pepper flakes

for meatballs and sausages
1 pound ground beef
¾ pound ground pork
¾ cup fresh bread crumbs, lightly toasted
¾ cup (3 ounces) grated Pecorino-Romano
1 bunch Italian parsley, minced
5 garlic cloves, minced

Kosher salt
Black pepper in a mill
2 eggs, beaten
Olive oil
8–10 Italian sausages, preferably hot

to finish
2 pounds dried spaghetti or spaghettini
Kosher salt
Red pepper flakes
Parmigiano-Reggiano, in one piece

Set the pork skins fat-side up on a work surface. Use a very sharp knife to slice off fat until there is just about ¼ of an inch left on the skin.

Turn the skins over, so the fat is face-down, and season all over with salt and pepper. Spread minced garlic over both skins, followed by lemon zest, parsley, and pine nuts.

Cut two pieces of twine, each about 36 inches long. Roll up one pork skin as tightly as possible. Set a string under one end, pull the string over the skin, and tie it tightly; cross the two ends of the string over to make an "x" about 2 inches from the first knot and tie again; continue until the entire pork skin is securely tied. Repeat with the second skin. (This portion is best achieved by two people, one to hold the skins tightly rolled as the other ties.)

Pour a little olive oil into a large, heavy, deep pot set over medium heat and, when it is hot, add the pork skin rolls. Cook, turning frequently, until they are evenly browned all over. Use tongs to transfer the rolls to a plate.

Next, make the sauce. Put the onion into the pan with the drippings from the pork rolls, set the heat on low, and cook until soft and fragrant, about 15 minutes. Add the garlic cloves and brown evenly on all sides. Use tongs to transfer the garlic to the plate with the pork skin rolls.

Season the onion generously with salt and pepper. Add the crushed tomatoes, the tomato paste, and 3 cups of water. Stir in the dried basil, oregano, and crushed red pepper flakes. Increase the heat to high and bring the tomato mixture to a boil. Reduce the heat to very low, use tongs to return the pork rolls to the pot, and simmer very slowly for 6 to 8 hours, stirring now and then. If the sauce ever seems too thick, thin with a little water.

About an hour and a half before you expect the sauce to be finished, make the meatballs. Put the beef, pork, bread crumbs, cheese, parsley, and garlic into a bowl and mix well. Season generously with salt and pepper, add the eggs, and mix thoroughly.

Divide the mixture into 12 equal portions. Use your hands to roll into balls, wetting your palms before forming each one.

Pour a little olive oil into a large, heavy sauté pan set over medium heat and, when it is hot, add the meatballs, cook for about 1 minute, and then gently agitate the pan and continue to cook until they are evenly browned and have firmed up a bit. Work in batches if necessary. Transfer all the meatballs to a platter. Use a fork to prick each of the sausages in several places and brown them in the pan. Transfer the sausages to the plate with the meatballs.

Gently add the sausages and meatballs to the pot. Do not stir.

Fill a very large pot two-thirds full with water, add 3 tablespoons kosher salt, and bring to a rolling boil over high heat. Quickly add the pasta and stir vigorously with a pasta fork or long wooden spoon until the water returns to a boil. Stir every 2 to 3 minutes until the pasta is done. To judge doneness, begin to taste the pasta about 60 seconds before the package instructions suggest it will be done. If it is too firm, cook 1 minute longer and taste again. Continue until the pasta is tender but has a bit of resistance at its core.

Warm one very large rimmed serving platter and one smaller platter.

While the pasta cooks, use long tongs to find and remove the pork rolls from the sauce. Set on a clean work surface. Let rest 5 minutes and then use kitchen shears to snip the twine. Cut the rolls into ¾-inch thick slices. Cover with aluminum foil.

Drain the pasta, but do not rinse it. Tip the pasta onto the large platter, top it with 3 ladles of sauce; toss gently to coat all the pasta thoroughly. Top with more sauce but do not toss. Arrange the pork skin rounds on top of the spaghetti.

Use a large, flat spatula or spoon to carefully remove the meatballs, one at a time, and set them on the other platter. Use tongs to transfer the sausages to a work surface; cut each one in half diagonally, and add to the plate with the meatballs.

Pour the remaining sauce into a bowl or pitcher.

Serve immediately, with the remaining sauce, the pepper flakes, the cheese, and a grater.

> ***To drink:*** Any full-bodied red wine works beautifully with this dish but I recommend something from Francis Ford Coppola Winery, such as, Diamond Collection Claret, Diamond Red Blend or Archimedes, a Bordeaux-style blend that is the winery's flagship wine.

Summertime Spaghetti & Meatballs

Serves 4 to 6

"Go have some Lady and the Tramp*," a friend urged when I said I'd finished this book. It took me a second and then, as the adorable image of the scrappy Tramp and demure Lady sharing a platter of spaghetti and meatballs in the classic Disney film came into focus, I smiled. The next time you want some* Lady & the Tramp*, use whatever meatballs you like; I prefer Roasted Garlic Meatballs (page 27). Occasionally I use Chorizo Meatballs (page 50) and finish the sauce with some fresh cilantro when I do.*

Meatballs of choice, hot
Kosher salt
1 pound spaghettini or other thin strand pasta

Summer Tomato Sauce (page 178).
Chunk of Parmigiano-Reggiano, Dry Jack, or similar hard grating cheese

After frying the meatballs, set aside and cover them to keep warm.

Fill a large pot two-thirds full with water, add a tablespoon of salt, and when the water reaches a rolling boil, stir in the pasta and cook according to package directions until just done.

Use the pan from the meatballs to make the sauce and when it is done, add the meatballs, cover, and keep warm.

When the pasta is fully cooked, drain it but do not rinse it. Transfer it to a bowl, add a couple of ladles of sauce, and toss to coat it thoroughly.

Divide among individual soup plates.

Divide the meatballs and remaining sauce among the portions and top with a little grated cheese. Serve immediately with the cheese and a grater.

To drink: Light-bodied red wine, such as Beaujolais, chilled, sparkling wine.

Halloween Spaghetti & Meatballs

Serves 6 adults, easily doubled

When I was growing up, Spaghetti & Meatballs was a Halloween tradition, likely because it was the only thing my mother knew I would eat, as I was always too excited to be in a costume to care about food. Now that I have a grandson, I have carried on the tradition, sort of. We've hosted several costume parties for his friends where I've made classic Spaghetti and Meatballs with black noodles and served it as Juicy Eyeballs with Blood & Worms. Everyone, save a couple of timid little girls, is delighted by the ghoulish dish. Sometimes, I stuff black olives with mozzarella to make it look even creepier.

Roasted Garlic Meatballs (page 27), cooked
Olive oil
1 small yellow onion, diced
3–4 garlic cloves, minced
Kosher salt
2 teaspoons dried oregano
1 teaspoon dried thyme
¼ teaspoon red pepper flakes, optional
¾ cup dry white wine

8 cups fresh tomato concasse (page 178)
    or 2 28-ounce cans crushed tomatoes,
    preferably Muir Glen brand
2 tablespoons double-concentrated tomato
    paste
1 pound long black spaghetti or spaghettini
2 tablespoons minced fresh Italian parsley
½–¾ cup Vella Dry Jack, grated on the
    smaller blade of a box grater

Prepare the meatballs and set them aside.

To make the sauce, pour a little olive oil into a deep sauté pan set over medium-low heat, add the onion, and sauté until limp and fragrant, about 10 to 12 minutes; do not let it brown. Add the garlic, sauté 2 minutes more, and season with salt. Stir in the oregano, thyme, and red pepper flakes, if using.

Increase the heat to high, pour in the wine, and cook until it is reduced to a scant ¼ cup. Stir in the tomato concasse or canned tomatoes, whisk in the tomato paste, and when the liquid boils, reduce the heat to low and simmer until the sauce thickens slightly, about 12 to 15 minutes. Taste, correct for salt, and stir in the parsley. Reduce the heat to very low, just enough to keep the sauce hot; cover the pan.

Fill a large pot two-thirds full with water, add a generous tablespoon of kosher salt, and bring to a boil over high heat. When the water reaches a rolling boil, add the pasta and stir with a pasta fork or long wooden spoon until the water returns to a boil. Cook according to package directions until just done.

Drain but do not rinse the pasta.

Gently reheat the meatballs if necessary.

Put the hot pasta into a wide, shallow bowl or platter and ladle about half the sauce over it; agitate or toss gently to distribute the sauce. Scatter the meatballs over the top and sprinkle with just a little cheese.

Put the remaining sauce in one bowl and the remaining cheese in another and offer with the rest.

To drink: Milk; Claret, Chianti, Montepulciano.

Italian Meatball Soup

Serves 6 to 8

You often see soups similar to this one called Wedding Soup, which makes it easy to assume that it is served at traditional weddings. But this is not the case; the name actually refers to the marriage of flavors, of meat and vegetables, in the soup. Some versions include pasta, others don't. I like the combination of textures provided by the little pasta known as acini di pepe, which is shaped like peppercorns.

The Meatball (page 24), Roasted Garlic
    Meatballs (page 27), or Fresh Herb
    Meatballs (page 45), without condiments
    or accompaniments
12 cups chicken broth, preferably homemade
Kosher salt
6 ounces acini de pepe or other small pasta
¾ pound young spinach leaves, young
    arugula, or trimmed chard, cut into
    1-inch wide slices

½ cup chopped fresh Italian parsley leaves
Black pepper in a mill
Juice of 1 lemon
3 ounces (¾ cup) grated Parmigiano-
    Reggiano or Dry Jack cheese
Ultra-premium extra-virgin olive oil, such as
    DaVero Olio Nuovo, optional

Make the meatballs but do not wrap them or roll them in bread crumbs; simply form them into small balls and set them on a baking sheet. Refrigerate for 30 minutes.

Pour the chicken broth into a large saucepan or soup pot, taste and season with salt. Bring to a boil over high heat, stir in the pasta, reduce the heat and simmer for 7 minutes, stirring now and then.

Carefully put the meatballs into the soup and simmer very gently for 7 minutes more. Add the greens, stir gently, and cook 3 minutes more or a tad longer if using chard. Cover and let rest for 10 minutes.

Add the lemon juice.

Taste the soup, season with several turns of black pepper and correct for salt, if needed.

Ladle into soup plates or bowls. Scatter cheese over each portion, drizzle with olive oil, if using, and enjoy right away.

Avgolémone & Kephtéthes Soupa

Serves 6 to 8

Kephtéthes are tiny meatballs, typically made of lamb, served in a tangy broth fragrant with lemon and velvety in texture. Be sure to combine hot broth and the egg mixture slowly so that they egg does not heat too quickly, in which case it will coagulate. There is no fix when this happens, except to strain the liquid, discard the cooked egg and begin again, which is both annoying and wasteful. This version is inspired by the various versions I've enjoyed over the years.

2 quarts (8 cups) meat or poultry broth or stock (see *Note* below)
¾ pound ground lamb
½ cup cooked white rice
Grated zest of 1 lemon
½ small onion, minced
1 egg, beaten

4 tablespoons chopped fresh Italian parsley
2 teaspoons Greek oregano, crumbled
Kosher salt
Black pepper in a mill
2 large egg yolks
Juice of 2 lemons (about ⅓–½ cup)

Make the broth or stock if you have not already done so. This can be done a day or two in advance.

To make the kephtéthes, put the lamb, rice, lemon zest, and onion into a bowl and mix well. Add the egg, half the parsley and oregano, and season generously with salt and pepper. Chill for 30 minutes.

Preheat the oven to 375 degrees.

Remove the meat mixture from the refrigerator and set a sheet pan next to a clean work surface.

Form small balls, about the size of a dime, and set them on the sheet pan. When all have been formed, set the baking sheet with the balls on the middle rack of the oven and cook for 8 to 10 minutes, until lightly browned and slightly firm to the touch. Remove from the oven.

To finish the soup, pour the broth or stock into a saucepan and warm over medium-low heat. Carefully add the kephtéthes, cover and simmer for 10 minutes; do not let the soup boil. Remove from the heat.

Put the egg yolks into a medium bowl and whisk vigorously until thick, frothy, and pale yellow. Add the lemon juice and whisk for another minute. Slowly drizzle in a ladleful of the hot stock, whisking all the while; whisk in a second ladleful, again very slow, and continue whisking until it cools slightly. The soup should be smooth and velvety, without lumps of cooked egg. Set aside briefly.

Use a slotted spoon to divide the little balls among individual soup bowls.

Slowly whisk the egg mixture into the soup. Taste for salt and pepper and stir in the remaining parsley. Ladle the soup over the kephtéthes and enjoy right away.

Alternately, serve in a soup tureen.

Note: You'll have the best results if you use homemade broth or stock. For the most delicate soup, use chicken broth. For a soup with richer flavors, use duck, veal, or beef stock or stock made with a combination of meats.

Appendix

Basic Recipes

Homemade Bread Crumbs

Makes about 2½ to 3 cups

It can be tempting to buy commercial bread crumbs, but unless you are selecting panko, the Japanese bread crumb, it's never a good idea. They are too dry, they soak up moisture and typically result in a dry meatball. If you have good bread past its prime but no time to make the bread crumbs, wrap it well and freeze it until you do have the time.

½ loaf sourdough or other hearth bread, about 2 days old

Cut or tear the bread into chunks and put a large handful into the work bowl of a food processor fitted with its metal blade. Pulse several times until the bread is reduced to crumbs. Transfer to a bowl or storage container and continue until all of the bread has been processed.

To toast the crumbs, spread them over a baking sheet and set them in a 250-degree oven for about 15 minutes or until they are lightly browned; use a spatula to turn them halfway through cooking.

Remove from the oven, cool, and store in a sealed container in the refrigerator.

Clarified Butter (Ghee)

Makes about 1 cup

It is important to use the best butter you can find, preferably butter from grass-fed cows. You also want butter with the highest percentage of butterfat, as this is indicative of quality. In the United States, butter must contain 80 percent butterfat and most come in at about 81 percent. Artisan butters and European butters are higher, typically around 85 percent. The remaining ingredients include water, whey, and milk solids, all of which lower the smoke point of the butterfat and must be eliminated through the process of clarification. If you do not live in dairy country where you have access to local butter, it is best to buy it unsalted, as it will be fresher than salted butters from large producers.

2 sticks (1 cup) butter, preferably unsalted

Put the butter in a small, heavy saucepan set over low heat. When the butter is fully melted, use a thin spoon to scoop off and discard any particles that have collected on the surface. Carefully pour the liquid butter into a wide-mouthed glass jar, leaving the whey and milk solids behind to be discarded. Cool the butter, cover, and refrigerate until needed. Clarified butter keeps for months.

Variations:
Ethiopian Spiced Butter: To ½ cup hot clarified butter, add ½ teaspoon each of cardamom seeds, fenugreek seeds, cumin seeds, ground turmeric, and dried oregano, along with 1 crushed and minced garlic clove and 1 teaspoon grated fresh garlic. Set over very low heat for 15 minutes and agitate the pan now and then. Remove from the heat and strain into a glass jar. Store, tightly covered, in the refrigerator several months.

Moroccan Smen: To ½ cup hot clarified butter, add 1 teaspoon dried oregano leaves and 1 teaspoon kosher salt, set over very low heat for 15 minutes and then strain into a glass jar. Store, tightly covered, in the refrigerator for up to 3 months.

Roasted Garlic Butter

Makes about ½ cup

Compound butters are butters with added ingredients; they form the foundation of countless classic recipes. The most familiar one is, of course, garlic butter. Roasted garlic butter is even better than classic garlic butter.

1 stick (½ cup) butter, preferably grass-fed organic butter, at room temperature

1 tablespoon roasted garlic purée (see recipe, page 176)

2 garlic cloves, pressed

1 teaspoon kosher salt

1 tablespoon chopped fresh Italian parsley

Put the butter into a small bowl, add the garlics, salt, and parsley and use a fork to mix until smooth.

To shape the butter into a log, set a piece of wax paper on a clean work surface and drop the butter into it. Wrap the butter loosely and then use the palm of your hand to shape it into a log by rolling it. Tighten the wax paper as it lengthens.

When the butter is an even log about 1¼ inches in diameter, set it, still in wax paper, on a sheet of plastic wrap and wrap tightly.

Freeze until ready to use.

The butter will keep in the freezer for about 3 weeks.

Variation:
Mustard Butter: Combine the room-temperature butter with 2 tablespoons Dijon mustard, 1 minced shallot, 1 minced garlic clove and 2 teaspoons chopped fresh Italian parsley. Season with salt and several turns of black pepper. Finish as described in the main recipe.

Roasted Garlic Purée

Makes about ½ cup

    Do not buy roasted garlic, which you see now and then in certain national supermarkets. It is very easy to make at home and will have a much better flavor when you make it yourself using the best garlic you can find.

3 large garlic bulbs, outer skins removed   Kosher salt
Olive oil   Black pepper in a mill

Preheat the oven to 325 degrees.

Rinse the garlic under warm water and try to remove the root; if it won't come out easily, clean it well to remove the dirt that collects there. Set the bulbs in a small, deep ovenproof dish (a small soufflé dish works well) and add about ¼ inch of olive oil, drizzling it over the bulbs as you pour. Add enough water to come up the sides of the garlic by about ½ inch. Season with salt and pepper, cover tightly with aluminum, set on the middle rack of the oven, and cook for 30 minutes.

Carefully test the garlic by pressing the fat part of a clove with your thumb; if it feels as soft as warm butter, it is done. If it is still firm, continue to cook until it is soft, testing every 10 minutes.

Remove from the oven, uncover, and let cool until easy to handle.

Set the garlic bulbs on a clean work surface and gently pull apart the cloves to expose their root ends. Use the heel of your hand to push out the pulp; if it is stubborn, remove the tiny bit of root that is attached to each clove.

Mash with a fork and transfer to a small bowl until ready to use.

Strain and reserve the cooking l to use as a sauce or in a sauce.

Tomato Concasse

Makes about 3 cups, easily doubled or tripled

Don't be intimidated by concasse, *which simply means that the tomatoes have been peeled, skinned, cored, minced, drained, and seasoned with a bit of salt.*

2 pounds vine-ripened beefsteak tomatoes   Kosher salt

First, sear and peel the tomatoes. To do so, spear a tomato through its stem end with a dinner fork and turn it over a high flame or hot burner as the skin blisters and pops. Set the seared tomatoes on a baking sheet.

When all the tomatoes have been seared, use your fingers to pull off the skins, beginning with the first one you seared, as it will have cooled enough to handle. Use a sharp paring knife to remove the stem cores.

Set a strainer over a deep bowl.

Cut the tomatoes in half through their equators, hold each over the strainer, and squeeze out the seeds and gel. Set the tomatoes aside. Stir the seeds and gel to release all the juice and then discard the seeds.

On a clean work surface, chop the tomatoes as finely as possible, reducing them nearly to a pulp.

Work in batches and transfer the chopped tomatoes and their juice to the strainer. When all the tomatoes have been chopped, add about a teaspoon of salt to them and let them drain, stirring every so often. What remains in the strainer is the tomato concasse. Transfer it to a bowl and season to taste with salt.

Reserve the juice for another use (it makes a great Bloody Mary).

Summer Tomato Sauce

Makes about 3 cups

This sauce is ideal during hot weather, when we don't want to have the stove on for long; it cooks in minutes. The time to make it is when you have ripe, local tomatoes from your own garden, a neighbor's garden, or a local farmers' market. When tomatoes are not in season, you should use a 14-ounce can of diced or crushed tomatoes, preferably Muir Glen brand. You should also omit the basil and use chopped Italian parsley instead.

3 cups Tomato Concasse (page 177)
3 tablespoons butter
2 fresh (not aged) garlic cloves, crushed and minced
Kosher salt

Black pepper in a mill
Red pepper flakes
1 tablespoon crème fraîche
4–5 basil leaves, cut into very thin strips

Make the tomato concasse.

Set a medium sauté pan over medium heat, add the butter and, when it is melted, add the garlic and sauté until it just softens, about 90 seconds. Add the concasse, heat through, and use a fork to break up any big pieces. Taste and correct for salt; add several turns of black pepper and a pinch or two of red pepper flakes.

If the sauce is too thick, add a bit of the reserved juice from the tomato concasse.

Stir in the crème fraîche, taste, correct the seasoning, and remove from the heat.

Stir in the basil and use within 30 minutes.

The Simplest Stove Top Chicken Stock

Makes about 8 cups

Once you have made chicken stock at home a time or two, you won't need a recipe. Vary this according to the season, to your preferences, and to what you have on hand or in the garden. If I have leeks or spring garlic, I add some of the green stalks. Sometimes I include ginger, sometimes I don't. Now and then I'll put in a few curls of lemon zest and occasionally I add hot chiles or spices, depending on the soup I'm planning to make. What I don't do is measure anything or think too much about it. To make the stock in a slow cooker, see the note that follows the main recipe.

1 local pastured chicken, rinsed
Chicken gizzard, heart and neck, if available
Kosher salt
1 onion or 2–3 shallots, trimmed
    and quartered

1–2 carrots, cut in chunks
3 or 4 Italian parsley sprigs
Bay leaf, optional
Several fresh ginger slices, optional
1 teaspoon white or black peppercorns

Season the chicken inside and out with salt and put it into a soup pot or large saucepan. Cover it with water and add the onion or shallots, carrots, parsley, bay leaf, and ginger, if using, and peppercorns.

Set over medium-high heat and, when the water just reaches a boil, cover the pot and remove it from the heat. Let sit for 1 hour.

Remove the chicken from the poaching liquid, set it on a platter, and let cool to room temperature. Cut or pull the meat from the bones, set the meat aside, and return the carcass, any bones you've pulled off, and any juices that have collected on the platter to the pot. Add the chicken skin to the pot, too. (Use the chicken meat to make salads, sandwiches, tacos, quesadillas, enchiladas, and pasta dishes.)

Set the pot over very low heat and simmer for several hours, until the bones have nearly disintegrated and the stock is flavorful. Top off with water as needed.

Cool, strain, and refrigerate; skim off the layer of fat that forms on top of the stock.

Chicken stock can be held in the refrigerator for 3 days and in the freezer for 3 to 4 months.

> **Note:**
> You can easily make this stock in a slow cooker, and if you have a stove that you don't trust leaving on overnight, this is the best technique. After removing the meat from the bones, put the bones into a slow cooker, add the poaching liquid, and set on high. When the liquid begins to simmer, reduce the heat to low and cook, covered, for 12 to 18 hours. Strain the broth into a clean container, cool, refrigerate, and remove the layer of fat on top of the cooled stock.

Beef Stock

Makes about 8 cups

The vinegar helps pull calcium and other valuable nutrients from the bones, so it is a good idea not to admit it.

Olive oil
3 pounds grass-fed beef, such as chuck, top
    round or trimmings, cut into chunks
Kosher salt
5 pounds meaty grass-fed beef bones
1 large yellow onion, skin on, halved
6–8 garlic cloves, skin on

1 medium carrot, cut into chunks
3 large tomatoes, cut in chunks, or 1
    14-ounce can of tomatoes, drained
Several Italian parsley sprigs
1 tablespoon black peppercorns
¼ cup red wine vinegar

Pour a thin film of olive oil into a large stockpot set over medium heat and, when the pan is hot, add the beef and sear for about 2 minutes or until it no longer sticks to the pan. Turn and continue until the meat is evenly browned all over.

Season with salt.

Add the bones, onion, garlic, carrot, tomatoes, and parsley and pour in 12 cups of water.

Add the peppercorns and vinegar, increase the heat to high and, when the mixture boils skim off any foam that collects on the surface of the liquid.

Reduce the heat to very low and simmer gently for several hours or as long as overnight; add additional water as needed to keep all the ingredients covered.

Do not stir.

Remove from the heat, cool, and strain into a large container. Chill, remove the layer of fat that collects on top. Use within 4 days or freeze for up to 4 months.

Basic Quinoa

Makes about 3 cups

Quinoa is an edible seed that is often misidentified as a grain. It is related to chard, beets, and spinach and in some regions of the world, especially South America, the leaves as well as the seeds are eaten. One of its benefits is that it is gluten free; it also functions similarly to certain grains, making it an excellent option for grain-type salads. It is also an ideal substitute for bread crumbs in meatballs. It has a protective coating that should be rinsed off thoroughly before cooking so that it does not contribute a bitter flavor to your meatballs.

1 cup quinoa, white or red   1 teaspoon kosher salt

Put the quinoa in a medium or large strainer and rinse it for several minutes under cool running water, agitating the quinoa all the while.

Shake off the excess water, transfer to medium saucepan, add 2 cups water and the salt, and bring to a boil over high heat. The moment the water boils, reduce the heat so that it simmers gently and cover the pan. Set a timer for 15 minutes.

When the timer goes off, reset it for 10 minutes, remove the quinoa from the heat, and do not lift the lid.

After 10 minutes have passed, lift the lid and use a fork to fluff the quinoa. Let cool and use immediately or refrigerate, covered, for 3 to 4 days.

Resources

When you search for ingredients, it is always best to start close to home, at locally owned stores and markets where the staff understand the ingredients they are selling and know their sources. It is very helpful to develop relationships with local farmers, ranchers and other produces who can often lead you to what you need even if they don't have it themselves.

This is, of course, not possible in every community and so I offer a few sources here for ingredients that can be hard to fine in some areas.

The Butcher Block Fresh Meat & Seafood

(702)558-6328

thebutcherblocklv.com

This excellent mail order retail source has caul fat, lamb, duck and a wide selection of other American meat, poultry and game.

DaVero

766 Westside Road

Healdsburg CA 95448

(707)431-8000

davero.com

When you need outstanding olive oils and vinegars and can't find them close to home, this is an excellent mail order resource, including for their handcrafted Italian-style wines.

Golden Gate Meat Company

San Francisco Ferry Building Marketplace, Shop #13

(415)983-7800

goldengatemeatcompany.com

A perfect resource for anyone living in the San Francisco Bay Area, this popular butcher shop also ships via FedEx overnight. They typically have caul fat, available by the pound, as well as a big selection of American meat, poultry and game, including lamb and duck.

Local Spicery

372 Bel Marin Keys Blvd., Suite G

Novato CA 94949

(415)382-6455

localspicery.com

Nick Davoren and Evelyn Wood's little company has a broad reach, as they ship their freshly milled spices nationally. They specialize in artisan blends, including berbere, but also sell dozens of single spices, herbs, dried chiles, rubs, salts and more. Their Spice Adventure Club makes a great gift.

METRIC AND IMPERIAL CONVERSIONS

(These conversions are rounded for convenience)

Ingredient	Cups/Tablespoons/Teaspoons	Ounces	Grams/Milliliters
Butter	1 cup=16 tablespoons= 2 sticks	8 ounces	230 grams
Cream cheese	1 tablespoon	0.5 ounce	14.5 grams
Cheese, shredded	1 cup	4 ounces	110 grams
Cornstarch	1 tablespoon	0.3 ounce	8 grams
Flour, all-purpose	1 cup/1 tablespoon	4.5 ounces/0.3 ounce	125 grams/8 grams
Flour, whole wheat	1 cup	4 ounces	120 grams
Fruit, dried	1 cup	4 ounces	120 grams
Fruits or veggies, chopped	1 cup	5 to 7 ounces	145 to 200 grams
Fruits or veggies, puréed	1 cup	8.5 ounces	245 grams
Honey, maple syrup, or corn syrup	1 tablespoon	.75 ounce	20 grams
Liquids: cream, milk, water, or juice	1 cup	8 fluid ounces	240 milliliters
Oats	1 cup	5.5 ounces	150 grams
Salt	1 teaspoon	0.2 ounce	6 grams
Spices: cinnamon, cloves, ginger, or nutmeg (ground)	1 teaspoon	0.2 ounce	5 milliliters
Sugar, brown, firmly packed	1 cup	7 ounces	200 grams
Sugar, white	1 cup/1 tablespoon	7 ounces/0.5 ounce	200 grams/12.5 grams
Vanilla extract	1 teaspoon	0.2 ounce	4 grams

OVEN TEMPERATURES

Fahrenheit	Celsius	Gas Mark
225°	110°	¼
250°	120°	½
275°	140°	1
300°	150°	2
325°	160°	3
350°	180°	4
375°	190°	5
400°	200°	6
425°	220°	7
450°	230°	8

Index

Resources